KILLING JESUS

OF NAZARETH

*According to a Trustworthy,
High View of Holy Scripture*

GORDON KENWORTHY REED

Tanglewood Publishing

KILLING JESUS OF NAZARETH

According to a Trustworthy, High View of Holy Scripture

By Gordon Kenworthy Reed

— ✝ —

***LOVINGLY, HUMBLY AND GRATEFULLY
DO I DEDICATE THIS BOOK***

*"Unto Him who loved us, and washed us from
our sins in His own blood."*

Beautiful Savior Lord of the nations!

Son of God and Son of Man!

*Glory and Honor, praise adoration,
now and forevermore
be Thine.*

CONTENTS

Publisher's Note

The purpose of this work is to give a correct Biblical account (i.e. what the bible actually says vs. what we think it says or want it to say) of the killing of Jesus of Nazareth. Factual reporting of the biblical narrative supports both the divine and human nature of Jesus through Jesus' own testimony, through the testimony of eyewitnesses, and through events described in the Bible which are associated with both of His natures.

In many instances in his book Bill O'Reilly differs and presents a view that is contrary to the primary source of the history of Jesus, the Bible. We only ask that you, the reader, give us the opportunity to present a view of Jesus which is not only a well-established one, but which has stood the test of time; does justice to what the Bible actually teaches; is supported by church historians, scholars, and theologians throughout the centuries; and is written about today by renowned Bible teacher and theologian, Gordon Kenworthy Reed.

On a personal note, the author and publisher agree that we like Mr. O'Reilly, and value his love of truth exhibited every evening on the O'Reilly Factor. We only wish that he had been more accurate with the primary source, The Bible, in writing about the killing of Jesus, regardless of his personal view of Holy Scripture. Since he wasn't accurate in all instances, we decided to include an Introduction, written by author and educator Paula Rodriguez, which clearly shows weaknesses and discrepancies in the O'Reilly book, as well as O'Reilly's understanding of the real purpose in Jesus' death.

THE PUBLISHER

Introduction

It seemed like such a great idea. My husband, who happens to be the publisher of this book, approached Rev. Gordon Reed with the idea for a book along the lines of Bill O'Reilly's Killing Lincoln and Killing Kennedy. The book could be called Killing Jesus of Nazareth. Rev. Reed liked the idea and got to work on it. Then a few months later, Bill O'Reilly announced his newest historical book in the works—Killing Jesus. At first it seemed redundant to have two new books on the market with virtually the same title. But the more we thought about it, the more we began to realize the tremendous differences that would exist between the two books.

When you are writing about something that actually happened, the details are what they are. You can't change those. The differences, and this is key, are in the interpretations of those facts. O'Reilly is trying to write his book from a totally secular, historical perspective. Reed is writing from a spiritual perspective. Yes, Jesus lived in a historical place and time, and His story was told by secular historians of the day. But Jesus was spiritual. He was and is God Himself. So it would be an injustice to ignore the spiritual aspects of His life and death. You can never understand His story otherwise.

The first problem with O'Reilly's book is its purpose. On page 4 of his book, O'Reilly says, "But the incredible story behind the lethal struggle between good and evil has not been fully told. Until now. At least, that is the goal of this book." However, on page 2, he has already said, "But this is not a religious book. We do not address Jesus as the Messiah, only as a man who galvanized a remote area of the Roman Empire and made very powerful enemies while preaching a philosophy of peace and love." In other words, Bill O'Reilly and his co-author Martin Dugard are going to explain the struggle between good and evil from a strictly historical perspective. What they have failed to realize is that without considering the God of the universe, there can be no concept of good and evil. There can be no standard for what should and should not be done. So their book is destined to fail in its stated goal simply because they have attempted the impossible—to explain spiritual, moral ideas through empirical, quantifiable methods. But that is not the only issue; there is also the question of how O'Reilly actually views Jesus.

Although Bill O'Reilly says that he is a Christian, and I will take him at his word on this, there are areas of the Christian faith and teaching with which he seems to have difficulty. The first of these areas is the authority of the Bible itself. We know from his interview with Roma Downey and Mark Burnett about their film The Bible that he believes that "a lot of the Bible is allegorical." He also is not sure of the historical accuracy of the Bible; he says in Killing Jesus, "Much has been written about Jesus, the son of a humble carpenter. But little is actually known about him. Of course we have the Gospels of Matthew, Mark, Luke and John, but they sometimes appear contradictory and were written from a spiritual point of view rather than as a historical chronicling of Jesus's life." [p. 1] In discussing his sources for the book, he says, "But putting together Killing Jesus was exceedingly difficult. We had to separate fact from myth based upon a variety of sources, some of which had their own agendas."[p. 273]

So what does he consider fact and what is considered myth? Apparently, the raising of Lazarus from the dead is a myth. "The legend of Jesus's raising of Lazarus from the dead became so widespread that it was a main component in the Temple priests' plotting against him."[p. 199]. But the belief that Mary Magdalene was a prostitute, although not supported directly in Scripture, is fact. " A vibrant young girl named Mary walks the streets of Magdala…She will grow up to be a prostitute, doing what she must do to survive."[p. 90] In discussing the roots of this belief, the story of the prostitute who anointed Jesus with perfume, he says, "Though Mary Magdalene is not mentioned by name in this story, it has long been the tradition of Christian teaching that it was she."[p. 144] So a story clearly told in the Gospels is a legend, but a story based on tradition is the truth. No wonder O'Reilly found it difficult to sort out fact from fiction.

O'Reilly also has no problem with changing the story of Jesus if the mood strikes him. In an interview with Norah O'Donnell on 60 Minutes, Sept. 29, 2013, "O'Reilly admits that some of his facts directly contradict the Bible and he stands by them." On page 16, in discussing the story of the Magi, O' Reilly says, "Herod sends the Magi on their way. His parting royal decree is that they locate the infant, then return to Jerusalem and tell Herod the child's precise location so that he can venture forth to worship this new king himself. The Magi see through this deceit. They never come back." In the Gospel of Matthew chapter 2, verse 12, we are told, "And being warned in a dream not to return to Herod, they departed to their own country by another way." Yes, the Magi saw through Herod's deceit—because of a warning sent from God. On page 81, speaking of the town of Nazareth, O'Reilly says, "But Jesus is not long for this small town. The holiness and magnificence of Jerusalem call to him." Jesus's visits to Jerusalem are described in the Gospels, and never do we read of him being in awe of the magnificence of the place. While in Jerusalem, Jesus worshipped, he taught, he healed, he cleansed the temple, he was received as a conquering hero, and he was condemned to die. He was not awestruck. Jesus did not need to be inspired by the holiness and magnificence of Jerusalem; he was and is the very personification of holiness and magnificence in and of Himself.

But wait, there's more. On page 139, O'Reilly tells us, "Four of the apostles are fisherman. Jesus has specifically singled out men from this calling because their job requires them to be conversant in Aramaic, Hebrew, Greek and a little Latin, which will allow them to speak with a wider group of potential followers." Yet Scripture portrays these men as uneducated. In Acts chapter 2, on the day of Pentecost, the people in Jerusalem are quoted as saying, "Are not all these who are speaking Galileans? And how is it that we hear, each of us in his own native language?" The fact that they were Galilean fishermen was an argument against their being able to speak other languages, not in favor of it.

Mr. O'Reilly also seems to be confused about who Jesus really was. In some sections of the book, he appears to believe that Jesus truly was and is the Son of God. On page 131: "This reading is a pivotal moment. The passage that Jesus reads refers to an anointed deliverer, a man both prophetic and messianic. He will set them free. Jesus is saying that it refers to him, right now...In essence, Jesus tells these men he has long known not only that he is the

Son of God but that their rejection of this claim will cause God to turn his back on them." Again on page 132: "Three times he has declared himself to be the Son of God, a blasphemous statement that could get him killed. Further on, on page 163:"'But what about you?' Jesus inquires. 'Who do you say I am?' Peter speaks up. 'You are the Christ, the son of the living God.' Jesus agrees. 'Blessed are you, Simon son of Jonah, for this was not revealed to you by man but by my heavenly father.'" These statements, along with others, seem to indicate that O'Reilly does view Jesus as the Son of God. Interestingly, in all of these statements, he is using as his source the Gospels, which he has previously declared to be contradictory and not "a historical chronicling of Jesus's life."

In other sections, O'Reilly seems not to be quite so sure about Jesus's divinity. On page 176 he suggests, "Whether knowingly or unknowingly, Jesus has led a life that is a continual fulfillment of Jewish prophecy...It could be argued that as he grew and learned Scripture, he intentionally began contriving his actions and words to mimic the prophets' predictions." And on page 177: "At the age of thirty-six, Jesus is clever enough to act out any prophecy...But Jesus would be a fool to ride a donkey into Jerusalem. That would be a death sentence. For while the prophets have been very specific about the way the king of the Jews would be born and live his life, they are just as clear about how he will die." On page 188, O'Reilly seems to indicate that Jesus's entire life has been one long political or social campaign: "He has long strategized about the words he will say at Passover and the effect they will have on his followers, both old and new. He knows that his claims of being a king will lead to his crucifixion. He will be sacrificed, just as surely as those countless Passover lambs. It is just a matter of when."

What O'Reilly fails to appreciate is that Jesus knew exactly when. And that it was all part of the plan of redemption for mankind. Jesus knew how and when he would die. He created the men who would mock and crucify him and the tree that provided the wood for the cross. He came to earth for that express purpose. He did not need to "strategize;" he was and is God and can see the hearts and minds of all people. He knew then and he knows now how each person will respond to him.

O'Reilly's biggest problem is that he does not appear to understand what Jesus's purpose on earth really was or what he actually accomplished. The book jacket tells us that "Killing Jesus…recounts the seismic, political and historical events that made Jesus's death inevitable." And in their book, the authors do tell us the facts about how Jesus died, they tell us what was going on in the world around him when he died; and they tell us why others wanted him dead. But they don't tell us the truth about why he died. Their arguments are that the world and its forces held control over Jesus the Nazarene and that those forces eventually led to his death.

In this book, Rev. Reed's argument is that Jesus, God the Son, holds control over all of the world and its forces. Jesus died according to His own plan, not as a victim of world events. O'Reilly says that in order to understand "what Jesus accomplished and how he paid with his life, we have to understand what was happening around him." No, Mr. O'Reilly, we don't. What we have to understand is that we are all sinful creatures who, for some unexplainable reason, God wants with him in heaven. In order to satisfy divine justice, that would require a perfect sacrifice—Christ Jesus, God the Son. So because of his infinite, unfathomable love, Jesus gave up the glory of heaven, came to earth as a man, and died an excruciating death on the cross to become our substitutionary sacrifice. And then he rose from the tomb, conquering death and evil once and for all. That, Mr. O'Reilly, explains the struggle between good and evil. And that is why Jesus died.

PAULA RODRIGUEZ, AUTHOR, EDUCATOR

Kovacs, Joe. "Bill O'Reilly: The Bible Contradicts Itself." WND Faith. 28 Feb 2013. http://www.wnd.com/2013/02/oreilly-proclaims-the-bible-contradicts-it-self/#7BwkhqGw1EGtMpZB.99

O'Donnell, Norah. "Killing Jesus." 60 Minutes Overtime. 29 Sep 2013. http://www.cbsnews.com

Prelude

He was alone, terribly alone. He was already condemned to die a painful and shameful death. He knew there was no escape, nor did He seek one. It was early dawn the last day of His life and the fulfillment of why He came to earth. The road ahead held for Him a sorrow and a horror too deep for words. He was to drink the dreaded cup from which he had earnestly and tearfully sought deliverance the night before and to which he had surrendered saying, "O my Father, if it be possible let this cup pass from Me; nevertheless, not as I will but as You will." These words were spoken in deep agony of spirit, for He knew what this surrender would cost Him. The darkness of soul through which he was now passing would give way to a darkness unimaginable. Yet three times He prayed this prayer, adding at the last; "My Father' if this cup cannot pass away unless I drink it, Your will be done."

As He spoke these last words, the stillness of the Garden of Gethsemane was broken by the growing sounds of marching feet and muttering men. The darkness gave way to the light of torches revealing the faces of those sent to arrest Him and bring Him to trial before the ruling body of the Jews, the Sanhedrin. The hatred He saw in the faces of those who came to arrest Him would be far surpassed when He would be brought by these guards into the presence of those who ordered His arrest.

This night had not started this way. Rather with his close and devoted disciples and friends, He had celebrated the last Passover
feast in which He would ever take part and the last Passover ever
that would hold any blessing or benefit for those who would par-
take. He had carefully observed all the ritual prescribed in the Torah, the Law of Moses. His disciples had followed His instructions
and carefully prepared for the feast. The innocent lamb had been
slain in the accustomed way and its body roasted according to the
law. The other elements of the feast were in order when Jesus and
His followers reclined to participate. He alone knew this would be
the last Passover feast of merit, so He instituted a new feast and a
new celebration. To this day His followers around the world celebrate and call to mind that feast of old and the amazing fulfillment
of it in His person and work. They await the day when He will join
us in this feast in the Father's kingdom.

Following the feast, He began to reveal to His disciples what lay
ahead, teaching, exhorting, and admonishing them in preparation
for His departure the next day. He gave them stern warnings and
at the same time comforting assurances and promises that would
sustain them in the hours, days, and years through which they
would pass. When He warned them of their weaknesses and failures, they all protested, especially Simon Peter. For Jesus had said,
"All of you will forsake Me." That was too much for bold Peter, who
responded to this warning by saying, "I will not forsake You, I will
lay down my life for You." Jesus answered, "Will you lay down your
life for Me? Truly I say to you, the rooster will not crow till you
have denied Me three times."

Before this night would end, the warning of Jesus to Peter was
fulfilled. It was one thing to boldly proclaim his loyalty and love
for Jesus in the comfort and light of the upper room where

they celebrated the Passover. But now in the lonely garden with darkness and danger all around him and Jesus forbidding him to defend Him with the sword, Simon's courage began to fail. Soon Jesus would be taken away for trial, and Peter would be left warming himself by the fire of those who hated his Lord and were determined to kill Him. Then what Peter thought and said could never happen and what Jesus warned him would happen, did happen. Brave bold Peter denied Him three times before the rooster announced the arrival of a new day. Upon the third denial, Peter came face to face with Jesus who had heard that last vehement denial and the loud cursing that accompanied it. Peter, overcome by shame and sorrow, stumbled off into the night bitterly weeping for his failure and sure that he would never see Jesus again alive.

The arresting officers took Jesus to the home of Annas, the High Priest emeritus of the Jews, and the father-in-law of the reigning High Priest Caiaphas. These were the two men who had the most power in Judea. They did not have the ultimate power of inflicting the death penalty upon Jesus or any other accused of capital crimes, but they did have considerable influence on the Roman Governor, Pontius Pilate, who did have that authority. They both hated Jesus with malicious and unrelenting determination to have Him killed. They hated Him for many reasons, but with unreasoning hatred and determination to put him to death. They saw Him as a threat to their power and position.

When Herod The Great had heard of his birth thirty some years before, he tried his best to have Him found and killed. He even went so far as to order the execution of all male babies from two years old and younger in his frantic but futile effort to kill Jesus. But where Herod had failed in his vain attempt to kill Jesus, Annas, Caiaphas and their many self-serving minions would succeed; or at least they thought they had succeeded when Jesus breathed His last agonizing breath on the cross.

There was only one purpose for arresting Jesus and going through the motions, flawed as they were, of a trial. For almost three years they had schemed and plotted to kill Him. When Jesus began His public ministry at the age of thirty, He had been endorsed and promoted by the most influential man in all Judea, John the Baptist. John had a huge following among the common people, and thousands flocked to hear him and to be baptized by him. The religious establishment, headed by Annas and Caiaphas, had been alarmed and angered by the message and methods of this fanatic, but were confused by his refusal to accept the Messianic role the people would have forced on him. However, John had made it very clear that though he was not the Messiah; yet the Messiah was close at hand, and he said of Him, "I am not worthy to untie the strap of His sandal". Then when John saw Jesus coming towards him, he said, "Behold the Lamb of God who takes away the sin of the world." By that proclamation, John had, in a sense, sentenced Jesus to death. He also added to his adulation of Jesus, "And I have seen and borne witness that this is the Son of God."

However, the religious establishment was spared the necessity of dealing with John because that bold Prophet of God had openly rebuked Herod the tetrarch of Galilee for his adulterous affair with his brother's wife and all his open immorality. For this bold witness John was arrested, cast into prison, and later executed. But John's endorsement of Jesus had prepared the way for many of the common people to look to Jesus with great expectations.

Almost immediately the Pharisees, Sadducees, the Priests, and the temple Scribes began to oppose all that Jesus taught and did; for they saw in Him and His teachings a real and serious threat to their own flawed interpretation of God's revelation and the possible end of their position and power. They were greatly alarmed at His obvious spiritual power as it was manifested not only in His powerful teachings but in His many undeniable miracles which seemed to authenticate His teaching. There were some honest and sincere men in the ranks of the religious establishment who believed that Jesus must be a messenger of God. One of their highest ranked scholars, Nicodemus, who was also a respected and influential member of the Sanhedrin, went to Jesus furtively to question Him; for the many signs and miracles Jesus performed testified that He was sent from God. But for this man or any other man of note who was a part of the religious establishment to take a strong stand for Jesus and His teachings would mean expulsion from even the local Synagogue as well as the ruling body of the Jews. The price would be very high, too high for most.

Another reason for the hatred of Jesus was His unforgivable act of publicly denouncing the lucrative (for the High Priest especially) practice of the Temple trade and the practice of exchanging money for a profit in the temple complex with the many pilgrims who made their way to the temple for the several feasts and celebrations of the Jews. Not only did He publicly denounce the practice, but even used force to expel those who ran these endeavors which had the endorsement of the priestly caste. Such an act could not only expose the evils of this practice, but could bring it to an end; and that would be a financial catastrophe for those who received such enormous profits from the temple trade.

Now Jesus was in their power. He had been arrested, His few frightened disciples dispersed. There was no one to stand with Him or for Him. At long last Annas and Caiaphas could do away with Him. They had even assembled some of their lackeys who would testify that He had led the people astray, had claimed the power to destroy the glorious temple and rebuild it in three days, and had committed all manner of blasphemy in claiming to be the Messiah. "Him, the Messiah? This man who spent most of His time with sinners and publicans? This man who had defied and disputed the accepted and traditional understanding of the Torah, God's holy law contained in the Mishnah, the wisdom of the centuries? This man whose power source was obviously the Prince of Evil? This man who had not asked permission from the ruling powers of Israel to preach and teach, even in the temple? Why, if this man claimed to be the Messiah he had better act like they expected Him to act, and do the things they thought he should do. This man now completely within their power and whose life was soon to be forfeited for all His crimes the Messiah of Israel? Utter nonsense! Why, if He really was the Messiah, He would be feeding the people constantly as Moses did during the exodus from Egypt, maybe even turning the stones into bread to feed them. If He was really the Messiah, He would have made a public display of His supposed power, maybe even casting Himself down from the pinnacle of the temple and having mighty Angels bear Him up lest he break his body in the fall. If He really was the Messiah, He would rise up and claim the Roman Empire for His own as well as all the other kingdoms and empires of this world. No! Their sacred duty required of them as God's High Priests to put this pretender, this false Messiah, to death. Maybe that would hasten the day when their true Messiah would come and fulfill all their dreams and meet all their expectations. So they proceeded with their "trial" of Jesus.

Annas, High Priest emeritus, began the proceedings by questioning Jesus concerning His disciples and His teachings. Jesus responded with these words: "I spoke openly to the world; always I taught in the synagogues and the temple where all the Jews come together. I said nothing in secret. Why do you question Me? Question those who heard me, they know what I said." Upon hearing these words one of the arresting officers slapped Jesus in the face saying, "How dare you answer the High Priests this way?" Jesus answered him, "If I have spoken wrongly testify of the wrong; but if I have spoken truly, why do you slap Me?" Wisely Annas sent Him in bonds to the reigning High Priest Caiaphas, who had also assembled together all the Sanhedrin.

Caiaphas had hastily assembled the Sanhedrin for this trial. He wasted no time because his schedule called for Jesus to be tried, found guilty, sentenced to death and sent to the Roman Governor, Pontius Pilate, to confirm the death sentence and proceed imme-diately with the execution before the Sabbath fell, which would have delayed the proceedings and possibly given time for some to come to the aid and defense of Jesus. Caiaphas had been too hasty and unwise in his selection of those called to testify against Jesus. Many false witnesses were eager to testify against Jesus but they kept contradicting each other and negating their effective-ness. It would seem ironic that Caiaphas was concerned about such a detail when the whole proceedings were blatantly irregular and unlawful. Then two more witness volunteered to testify they had heard Jesus brag that He would destroy the temple of God made with hands (which had taken 40 years already and was still in process) and in three days raise up a new temple. But even these two conspirators kept contradicting each other in their testimony. Caiaphas faced a dilemma; his plans were unraveling before his very eyes and ears. So he took over the proceedings and confront-ed Jesus with his own questions. To these questions Jesus made no response at all. Caiaphas was beginning to lose his temper because

23

his plans were in danger of falling apart. "Will you not answer these accusations and respond to these who witness against you?" Jesus remained silent.

Then Satan took complete control of Caiaphas. "Tell us" he screamed in the face of Jesus, "are you the Messiah, the Son of the Blessed? I adjure you by the living God tell us if you are the Messiah, the Son of God?" Caiaphas was sure now that he had placed Jesus in an impossible situation. If He said "no", then he would confess that he was a phony who had led the people astray and had borne false witness about Himself thus making himself liable to the death penalty. But if He said "yes", He would be guilty of the worst sort of blasphemy; and this too would condemn him to death. He had him at last and there was no way he could escape death, reasoned Caiaphas. Jesus' response was straight forward and true. "It is as you have said; I AM." The whole righteous assembly looked upon Him stunned. Here He was in bonds, subject to their authority and facing now sure death, with no power or possibility of living out the day, yet claiming for Himself identity with God. Jesus knew their thoughts so He added to His testimony: "Furthermore I say to you all, hereafter you will see the Son of Man sitting at the right hand of power and coming upon clouds of heaven."

Then in a hypocritical display of righteous indignation, Caiaphas tore his robes screaming, "He has spoken blasphemy. Why do we need more witnesses? You have heard his blasphemy. What is your verdict?" They all agreed to condemn Him worthy of death. The court was recessed until dawn just to make His condemnation "legal." Then followed the unbelievable scene which makes the condemnation of Jesus by the high court nothing less than a "legal" lynching. These holy men began to abuse Him by spitting in His face, beating Him with their fists while his hands were tied and he was defenseless. They blindfolded Him and continued beating Him and mocking between the blows saying, "Prophesy to us, Messiah, who is it who struck you?" At the same time they were speaking unspeakable blasphemy against Him. Their blasphemy and cruelty would continue when He was at last crucified by the decree of Pontius Pilate, the Roman Governor.

When dawn came and the new day began probably less than an hour later, the Sanhedrin was officially convened to pronounce sentence upon Jesus, and have their verdict confirmed by Pilate. He must have been truly a sad and pathetic sight, deserted, forsaken, denied and betrayed by His friends, savagely beaten and mocked; but He found no sympathy from these determined and angry men. They asked Him to repeat His confession now that the court was officially and legally convened. They put Him in the dock and asked again saying, "If you are the Messiah, tell us." Jesus responded, "If I tell you, you will not believe, and if I ask you, you will not answer. But from now on the Son of Man shall be seated at the right hand of the power of God." They all asked Him saying. "Then you are the Son of God?" He simply said, "Yes I am." At those words, the "trial" ended. They all agreed that He was guilty of a capital offense. "We need no further witnesses, for we have heard Him condemn Himself". The verdict was unanimous by all present. This man Jesus must die. All of His great teachings, all of His many miracles of healing and power, all of his deeds of mercy and kindness, none of these things meant anything to the High Court of the Jews. They had but to go through the formality of securing permission from the Roman Governor, Pilate, to proceed with the execution, preferably by crucifixion.

How could this possibly have happened? Why was He so hated and completely rejected? When one considers the many thousands of people who had been touched by His loving ministry and the apparent fervent conviction on the part of a small but loyal band of followers, it seems incredible and even impossible that He should be so alone and condemned. Why? How was it possible? Why had He not called upon the armies of heaven to come to His rescue? He had been condemned to death for telling the truth, when a very understandable lie might have saved His life. The answer to all these questions may only be found by going back to the beginning of all things. The answer begins in the ancient Garden of Eden, and continues to unfold throughout the long history of the human race as found in sacred scriptures. The answer is found in the developing story of the suffering and death of Jesus and is at last fully explained by the events following His suffering and death. Do you really want to know? Are you willing to walk with me as we diligently search for the answer?

1

Beginning of the Battle

"Back in Genesis 3:15, God had prophesied that there would be a continuing conflict between the descendants of Eve, and the descendents of the serpent (a struggle that would reach its climax at the cross.)…While the story of Cain and Abel is to be understood as historical, yet it also symbolizes the age-long conflict between good and evil, right and wrong and between the seed of the woman and the seed of the serpent."

Thus in his excellent commentary on the book of Genesis, Dr John D. Currid points to the inevitable connection between the fall of mankind and the killing of Jesus of Nazareth, apart from which the story of the murder of Jesus cannot be fully understood. More specifically the consequences of the fall into rebellion and sin by our first parents was the reason why their son Cain murdered their son Abel. This is a prototype of the killing of Jesus, and in many ways is somewhat similar. But before getting into these remarkable similarities, a closer look at Genesis 3:15 and associated verses is in order.

"The Lord God said to the serpent, because you have done this…I will put enmity between you and the woman and between your offspring and her offspring; he shall bruise your head, and you shall bruise his heel." The word enmity is a strong word, suggesting extreme hostility and murderous anger. Before long Abel was to experience this enmity to the point of murder at the hands of his brother Cain. Much, much later this enmity was to express itself in the hatred and murder of Jesus.

It is obvious from the context that the two lines suggested in Genesis 3:15, (the seed of the serpent and the seed of the woman), were not biological but spiritual. The offspring of the serpent (really Satan) are the spiritual children of Satan; those who choose to reject God, and give in to evil, and the evil One. Such was Cain who gave in to his fallen nature, rejected the sovereignty of God, ignored His advice and warning, and finally killed his own brother. The opponents of Jesus followed the same pattern, which led Jesus to warn them that their father was the devil. He (the devil) controlled their reaction to Jesus: which like Cain before them led them into enmity to the point of murder, thus proving they were the "seed of the serpent" and doing his will.

Now back to the story of Cain and Abel. They were obviously biological brothers, but spiritually they were from very different lineage. The Apostle John referred to Cain as being "of the evil one." Spiritually he was the "seed of the serpent." They grew to manhood under the guidance of their parents, Adam and Eve and would have been taught the same truths about God and His revealed will. They probably were both reminded of the fall, and of God's judgment and His warnings. Presumably, they were both taught by their parents the need to worship God and to offer to Him sacrifices worthy of Him. Cain had chosen to be a "tiller of the ground", a farmer, while Abel was a shepherd.

It was in the acts of worship that the differing lineage began to show itself. It may be too much of a stretch to say that Cain's offering was rejected because it was not a blood offering, because we

28

simply do not know what the Lord had revealed concerning the nature of their offerings. But what we do know was that the spirit in which they brought their offerings to the Lord revealed much of their spiritual conditions and natures. Cain brought to the Lord the fruit of the ground, while Abel brought the first born of his flock and the best part from the best beasts. By what manner the Lord revealed that He was pleased with Abel and his offering, we are not told. Nor are we told in what manner He revealed His displeasure with Cain and his offering. We are told, however, that God accepted Abel and his offering, but rejected Cain and his offering. Two New Testament passages help us understand the reasons.

In Hebrews 11:4 we read: "By faith Abel offered to God a more acceptable sacrifice than Cain, through which he was commended as righteous, God commending him by accepting his gifts." By faith Abel accepted God's promises and His requirements. This means that by faith Abel was a righteous man, yet knowing he was a sinner his offering was for sin and forgiveness, so he offered to God the sacrifice of faith and then the offering which indicated his faith. There is every indication that Cain's attitude of heart was not right with the Lord, nor did he come before God in faith and with a repentant heart. I John 3:12 reads: "We should not be like Cain who was of the evil one and murdered his brother. And why did he murder him? Because his own deeds were evil and his brother's righteous."

A word is in order to those who understand the story of Cain and Abel to be an allegory of the conflict between good and evil, right and wrong, rather than an actual incident. Good and evil are not just philosophical concepts floating around out there somewhere; they are descriptions of both attitudes and actions in human beings. So if you choose to regard this historical account as an allegory, then you are forced to find another historical event in which right and wrong, good and evil are demonstrated.

At this point we may observe some remarkable similarities between the killing of Abel and the killing of Jesus. The conflict between the two brothers was indeed a demonstration of the reality of conflict between good and evil. There will always be similarities whenever and wherever such conflicts exist. The comparison between the killing of Abel by Cain and the killing of Jesus by His contemporaries reveals some striking similarities, both in the people involved and in the actions taken by the "seed of the serpent." Both Cain and Abel were biological descendents of Adam and Eve, but it becomes obvious as the story develops that spiritually Cain was truly of the serpent's seed, and it is equally obvious that Abel was of the seed of the woman. How is this difference also seen in the murder of Jesus?

That Jesus was the seed of the woman is affirmed in the Scriptures. In fact, He was the promised seed in a very unique way, having conceived by the Holy Spirit and born of the Virgin Mary, even as the Prophet Isaiah had foreseen, but this is another story to be developed later. The comparison just on a human level is clearly seen. Both Abel and Jesus were righteous men. Every reference to Abel in the bible affirms that he was indeed a righteous, good man who honored God. Two such references are sufficient to demonstrate this. In Matthew 23:35, we read these words of Jesus when He was rebuking and warning the religious leaders of His day for rejecting Him: "...so that on you may come all the righteous blood shed on earth, from the blood of innocent Abel to the blood of Zechariah…whom you murdered…". The other reference is found in the book of Hebrews, 11:4; "By faith Abel offered to God a more acceptable sacrifice than Cain, through which he was commended as righteous, God commending him by accepting his gifts. And through his faith, though he died, he still speaks."

As for references which describe Jesus as a righteous man, they abound. For our purposes we will only look at a very few, especially when these words come not from His ardent followers, but from neutral and even hostile sources. The first of these is found in the Gospel of John, chapter 3. In the early days of His earthly ministry Jesus was approached by a very prominent religious leader who came to Jesus with words of commendation and a sincere desire to understand His teachings. "Rabbi, we know that you are a teacher come from God, for no one can do these signs that you do unless God is with him." This was high praise indeed coming from a man who was a part of the entrenched religious establishment which opposed Jesus at every turn. But even more amazing are the words of the Roman governor, Pontius Pilate, who eventually gave in to the demands that Jesus be sentenced to death. But before yielding to the demands of the religious leaders, he affirmed three times that Jesus was innocent of any crime. Moreover Pilate's wife sent him word during the trial saying: "Have nothing to do with that righteous man for I have suffered much because of him today in a dream." Even Jesus' betrayer recognized that the Lord was truly righteous, when upon attempting to undo his nefarious deed, Judas said, "I have sinned in that I have betrayed innocent blood."

The most amazing testimony of Jesus' innocence and His righteousness may be found in the words of a man who was crucified along with Jesus. He with another malefactor was put to death for crimes he had committed. When his comrade in crime began to rail against Jesus saying; "Are You not the Messiah? Save Yourself and us", he rebuked his fellow criminal with these words; "Do you not fear God, since you are under the same condemnation? And we indeed justly, for we are receiving the due reward of our deeds; but this man has done nothing wrong". Then he added, "Jesus remember me when You come into your kingdom."

Cain hated Abel to the point of murder because Abel was a righteous man, who pleased God, and Cain himself was not a righteous man, and neither he nor his offering pleased God. So instead of repenting of his sins, he blamed Abel for his rejection and his jealousy became hatred and his hatred led to murder. Jesus was hated by his adversaries of the religious establishment because by word and deed He proved that God was well pleased with Him. In contrast His enemies, the leaders of the established religion were powerless to do what Jesus did, and they had obviously perverted the revealed truth which came from God. Jesus spoke with clarity and with authority, and challenged their perverted misunderstanding of God's word. On at least two occasions God the Father affirmed that Jesus was truly speaking with His authority and commanded His disciples to "hear Him!"

That Jesus possessed extraordinary power was never denied even by His most bitter foes in the Jewish ruling body, the Sanhedrin. One of their number, Nicodemus, called "The Teacher in Israel", said to Jesus in a private interview, "Rabbi, we know that you are a teacher come from God, for no one can do these signs that you do, unless God is with him." Much later it seems that this man, Nicodemus may have become a believer in Jesus.

As Jesus' ministry continued, He demonstrated over and over again that truly "God was with Him". Once again He came under vicious attacks by the establishment who even foolishly claimed that He exercised power over the evil spirits by the father of evil, Satan himself. His opponents could not deny that He had performed marvelous works and miracles of healing unprecedented. For instance they never denied that He had opened the eyes of the blind, cleansed the lepers and even raised the dead. When Jesus asked them for which of His good works were they planning to stone Him, their answer revealed that they recognized His good works but did not recognize His claim to be God's Son. They did not deny that Jesus had raised Lazarus from the dead after he had been dead four days, but their answer to that undeniable miracle was a plot to kill both Jesus and Lazarus.

Humanly speaking and in a limited sense, Abel and Jesus were both murdered for the same reason; their righteousness exposed the unrighteousness of their enemies, and aroused their bitter hearts to hatred and murder. Truly the "seed of the serpent" regarded both righteous men as deadly enemies to be eliminated at any cost. One final comparison is in order. The true testimony of both righteous men out lived their death, and in the case of Jesus His death, as linked with His resurrection was His greatest victory.

2

Conflict Continued

Following the sad death of Abel, and the exile of his brother Cain, the murderer, the story of conflict between the "seed of the serpent" and "the seed of the woman" continued even as God had forewarned. There is much we do not know about these early days of mankind, but we are given a broad outline of the story and much of the focus of these early records is on this ongoing conflict. How many children were born to Adam and Eve, we are not told, but we are told about the one through whom the "seed of the woman" would be perpetuated, according to God's promise. Before considering this story of the promised "seed of the woman" we note that the "seed of the serpent" was also continued through Cain and his descendents. The curse of Adam's sin and the resulting fallen nature of mankind soon became apparent. The murderous sin of Cain was repeated in one of his heirs, Lamech, who also broke the creation ordinance of marriage between one man and one woman by taking to himself two wives. He displayed contempt for God's law in wanton slaying of any and all who got in his way or offended him. If God declared a seven fold vengeance of anyone who would murder Cain, Lamech threatened a seventy-seven fold vengeance on anyone who offended him and he apparently carried out his threat! So the "seed of the serpent" was being perpetuated in fallen humanity.

However the other side of the story, the "seed of the woman" was also presented. After so many years, at the age of 130 Adam and Eve had another son, whom they recognized as the fulfillment of God's gracious promise they had received even in the dark hours of their fall and God's confrontation with them. They named their son Seth, which means the "Appointed One" because they were convinced God had given them a son to replace slain Abel, the Righteous. It would be through the lineage of Seth that the true "Appointed One, the "Seed of the Woman" would one day come and fulfill the promise of God that He would crush the serpent's evil head.

The rapid growth of evil in the ancient world reached such deplorable depths that the "seed of the serpent" overwhelmed the "seed of the woman." Eventually it came to the point that God said of fallen humanity: "The wickedness of man was great in the earth, and that every intention of the thoughts of his heart was only evil continually…and it grieved Him to His heart". Then God decreed a universal flood that would bring total destruction of mankind, as well as the death of all animal and bird life on the earth. (The consequences of sin are always far more outreaching and deadly than we may ever imagine.) "But Noah found grace in the eyes of the Lord." The one remaining "seed of the woman" would survive, and to him and his family God would show amazing and saving grace. The subsequent story of the Flood, the Ark, and the sparing of Noah and his heirs is a thrilling story of God's intention and ability to fulfill the promises made to Adam and Eve in the long ago Garden of Eden.

There are of course many analogies and comparisons which could be pointed out between the story of the flood and the escape of Noah, and the killing of Jesus of Nazareth. But now we come to the story of Abraham. In which story we will find the incredible account of Abraham's faith and the offering up of his one and only true son, Isaac in obedience to God's command. Abram, (as Abraham was first called until God changed his name), was the tenth generation from Noah's son Shem, the godly seed. By this time the human race had become corrupt and rebellious once again, but God had already promised that He would never again destroy the world with a flood. Instead of preserving the "seed of the woman" by judgment upon the "seed of the serpent" God chose to preserve the righteous seed by selecting Abram to begin a new nation of people. This nation was chosen to preserve the godly seed until the true "Seed of the woman" would come. This One would be the Savior and redeemer God had promised long before in the Garden of Eden. He would be the One who would crush the heel of the serpent and end forever his evil determination to defile God's creation.

Terah, Abram's father had settled in a Chaldean city called Ur. But God called Abram to leave his father's household and go to a new land of which God would show him. "Go from your country and your kindred, and your father's house." This was not a suggestion but rather it was a command that Abram must obey. The command also contained a glorious promise. "And I will make of you a great nation, and I will bless you and make your name great, so that you will be a blessing. I will bless those who bless you and him who dishonors you I will curse, and in you all the families of the earth will be blessed."

Abram's immediate response was faith and obedience prompted by faith. This would become a pattern of his life. He was far from perfect, and at times his faith wavered and his obedience faltered, but God persevered in him and he became the spiritual father of all who by faith experience the grace of God. He set out for the land of Canaan at the age of 75, his wife being 65. It seems strange and ironic that he would go there of all places. The Canaanites, the descendants of wicked Ham, Noah's mocking son were there in the land. Yet it was in that place, surrounded by those people that Abram was to find his home and thus begin that special, chosen people through whom the promised One would come who would finally crush the serpent's head. Truly the ways of the Almighty are not our ways nor are His thoughts our thoughts.

Upon arriving there the Lord who led him there came to Abram and said: "To your seed I will give this land." Abram's faith was demonstrated both by following the leading of the Lord and also by building altars by which he would worship the Lord and be often reminded of God's commands and even more of God's constant grace and care. The best commentary of this man and his faithful obedience to the Lord is found in the book of Hebrews, chapter 11 verses 8-10. "By faith, Abraham obeyed when he was called to go out to a place that he was to receive as an inheritance. And he went out, not knowing where he was going. By faith he went to live in the land of promise, as in a foreign land, living in tents with Isaac and Jacob, heirs with him of the same promise. For he was looking forward to the city that has foundations whose designer and builder is God."

However, his story takes a strange turn. His faltering faith led him not only into Egypt, but into practices of untruthfulness and deceptions which did not honor God. But God did not turn His back on Abram. His repentance and strengthened faith is obvious as he left Egypt behind. He returned to the land of promise, renewed his faith and commitment to God and His will and enjoyed the blessings of God. God also renewed and expanded His promise to Abram of the land for his possession, but also of a great multitude of descendants. These promises have two dimensions. Abram and Sarai (later on God would change her name too) his wife will have a son who will be the heir of all promises made to Abram. The greater dimension of God's promises is seen in the vast multitudes of people to whom Abram would be their spiritual father and eventually the possessors of the promised new creation. This dimension would go far beyond the earthly fulfillment since Abraham was looking towards that eternal land and city over which the blessed "Seed of the woman" would rule and reign for eternity. "For he (Abraham) was looking forward to the city that has foundations whose designer and builder is God." There are those who steadfastly claim that the "seed of Abraham" applies only to the Jewish race and nation, and therefore the Promised Land is Canaan and Canaan only. However, the Apostle Paul made the bold statement in Galatians 3:29 "If you are Christ's, then you are Abraham's offspring, heirs according to the promise." So we too "are looking forward to the city that has foundations whose designer and builder is God." The true and perfect "Promised Land" is the new creation won for us by Christ through His death and resurrection.

Once more God came to Abram with the renewal of His amazing, but as yet unfulfilled promises. In this encounter God speaks; "Fear not Abram, I am your shield and great will be your reward." But Abram's responded with doubt and disappointment. "O Lord, what will you give to me since I am childless and my only heir is my servant Eliezer? God had promised him innumerable descendants, but so far he had none. Once more God assured Abram that he would have an heir from his own body, and that his descendants would be as innumerable as the stars in the heavens. In spite of the seeming impossibility of fulfillment given the age of Abram and his wife and her barrenness, we read these words: "Then he believed in the Lord; and He reckoned it to him as righteousness."

39

The battle was not over. Still "Sarai, Abram's wife had borne him no children". She decided to take matters into her own hands and persuaded Abram to take her maid, Hagar the Egyptian as another wife, and hopefully have children by her. What a golden opportunity Abram had and missed to demonstrate his faith to his doubting wife Sarai. Instead he readily gave into to Sarai's suggestion and more readily took Hagar. Almost immediately this servant girl Hagar became pregnant by Abram and began to mock and belittle Sarai's inability to conceive. She, with Abram's consent' drove Hagar away into the wilderness. But God interceded and by his angel ordered Hagar to return and submit to Sarai with the promise she will have a son and following him a long line of descendents. And as God revealed to Hagar before the birth of that child He became "A wild donkey of a man, his hand against everyone and everyone's hand against him, and he dwelt over against all his kinsmen."

Thirteen years later, when Abram was 99 years old, the Lord appeared to him once more saying to him, "I am God almighty, walk before me and be blameless that I may make My covenant between Me and you and may multiply you greatly." During that dramatic and truly life changing encounter, the Lord changed Abram's name to Abraham, the name by which we know him even today. But for the first 99 years of his life he was known as Abram. (Thankfully he did not live in this modern era with all the complications of name change we face. Think of the complications with bank accounts, phone numbers, Social Security and the IRS he would have faced.) The significance of the name change is related to the fulfillment of the earlier promise that God would make of Abraham a great nation through which all the earth would be blessed. In this present encounter God explicitly promised Abraham and Sarah (her name was changed too) that they would have a son in their old age and his name would be Isaac which means laughter. The seed of

Abraham and Sarah would be the continuation of the promised "seed of the woman" and through him, Isaac, the true "seed of the woman" would one day come forth. The incredible promise was fulfilled. Abraham and Sarah at the ages of one hundred for Abraham and ninety for Sarah became the parents of Isaac. The line of the "seed of the woman" would be continued down through the ages until at last the true Seed of the woman would be born of a virgin many centuries later. So Isaac was born and the cup of joy of Abraham and Sarah was full.

Then later there was a meeting between God and Abraham. It happened this way. I like to think this meeting was at night as an earlier meeting had been when God made the promise that Abraham would be blessed with many descendents. When Abraham expressed doubts because of his age, God said to him; "Look now to the heavens and count the stars if you are able to count them. And He said to him, 'thus shall be your progeny'". Later God added these words to that promise; "I will multiply your descendents as the sand which is on the seashore." I think Abraham's favorite time to commune with God would be when he could see the stars above and be reminded of God's promise. So now God came to Abraham, calling him by his new name which God Himself had given. "Abraham," God called. (It is one thing to have a general but casual relationship with another person, but when that relationship becomes personal and closer, then the conversation includes a name.) Abraham's trusting response was, "here I am." That answer implied more than mere location, It implied readiness to hear and obey. Probably Abraham was thinking "What new promise or command does God have for me now." The call of God had always meant blessing and often times very specific guidance' so he awaited the word of the Lord with eagerness to receive and to obey His word.

41

"Take now your son, your only son Isaac, whom you love and go to the land of Moriah and offer him there as a burnt offering on one of the mountains of which I will tell you." This command was startling and staggering. How can it be? This son is the son of promise through whom God had promised Abraham that He would make him the Father of a great people. This was the son given by God to Abraham and his wife Sarah when they were old and well passed child bearing years. This son was the beginning of the fulfillment of the promise that through Abraham and his seed, all nations would be blessed. And now God commands Abraham to slay his son and give up his body to the flames as a burnt offering to the Lord? How many times in the past had Abraham killed a lamb as a burnt offering to God? The ritual was simple. A perfect lamb, free from any defect was taken and by the hand of Abraham his throat would be cut and then the dead body would be cut into pieces and burned before the Lord as an offering to expiate sin. For a shepherd (and Abraham was a shepherd) this not only meant an economic loss, but an emotional wound as well. Good shepherds loved their sheep and especially their little lambs, and Abraham was a good shepherd. But now God has required him to do the same with his precious son Isaac.

No doubt a battle within his heart was now joined. The covenant that God had made with Noah was a perpetual covenant and included in this covenant was strict prohibition against murder, with a promise of dire punishment if murder was committed. Of the immediate command to offer Isaac as a burnt offering there could be no doubt. Could it be that Abraham had not heard God correctly? No, the voice was too clear, the command too direct. If Abraham denied this command, then all his past dealings with God would have to be called into question. Even as God had said, "... your only son Isaac, whom you love" so Abraham truly loved and cherished his son. By early morning the battle had been won and Abraham prepared for that fateful journey to the land of Moriah. Of course he did not tell Sarah the purpose of the trip, or why he would take Isaac with him; he could not.

The book of Hebrews answers the question, "How could Abraham possibly obey such a command?" "By faith Abraham, when God tested him, offered Isaac as a sacrifice. He who had received the promises was about to sacrifice his one and only son. Even though God had said to him 'it is through Isaac that your offspring will be reckoned.' Abraham reasoned that God could raise the dead, and figuratively speaking, he did receive Isaac back from the dead." Even so, this good and faithful man went on his journey of faith with his son Isaac and with a heavy though obedient heart. It is beyond difficult to image the agony and inner pain through which Abraham was going, but early the next morning, carefully making preparations for the offering, he took Isaac and two of his servants and set out for the land of Moriah. It was a three day journey to the appointed place but Abraham knew when he had arrived and leaving the servants with the donkey upon which he had ridden, he took Isaac his son and set out for the mountain God had shown him.

As the two walked on together, father and son, Isaac raised the natural question when he asked; "My father," and Abraham said, "Here I am my son." And Isaac asked; "Look we have the fire and the wood, but where is the lamb for the burnt offering?" It was a natural question to ask, and one Abraham knew was coming. "God will provide for Himself the lamb for the burnt offering" was his answer. Trusting Isaac accepted his father's explanation and the fateful journey continued until they arrived at the place of which God had told him. The stones were gathered, the wood arranged and it was revealed to Isaac he was to be the sacrificial lamb. He was tightly bound, laid atop the wood, and Abraham took out his knife, prepared to kill his son, his only son Isaac whom he loved, the son of God's promise, the son through whom a great nation would be born. The deed was almost done the knife was raised, the blinding tears fell upon his son's innocent face, mingling with the perplexed tears of fear shed by young Isaac. Up came the knife, the stroke must be sure and true, but it never fell upon the exposed throat of Isaac. Instead the voice of the Lord called to Abraham from heaven saying; "Abraham, Abraham." And he answered back once more, "Here I am." Three days before when this whole drama began God had called to Abraham, and Abraham had used the same words; "here I am". Then and now the words of his answer meant the same thing; "Here I am, ready to obey and to do Your will." Yes, even to sacrifice his son, his only son whom he loved so very much. "Withdraw your hand, do not harm the lad. For now I know you reverence God, since you have not withheld your son, your only son from me." It was not as if God did not know this before the test, but now Abraham himself knew that he truly loved the Lord his God with all heart, soul, mind and strength, and he was totally surrendered to His will.

The knife intended to take the life of Isaac, now was used to release him from the bonds and from death. Ever as Abraham had promised Isaac, God provided himself the substitute for the lad. There in nearby bushes a ram, a male sheep was entangled by his horns in the thick bush and the briars. Together, Abraham and Isaac capture the God-provided sacrifice and quickly it, and not Isaac becomes the sacrifice God had required of Abraham. Together, father and son worshiped the Lord through the means God had provided. Surely both men more fully understand the reason for such an act, and undoubtedly now had a deeper understanding than ever before of God's grace and mercy. How long they stayed at that blessed site we are not told, but there must have been a reluctance to leave that blessed place of God's provision. They gave that place a name, "God Provides" and that name serves as a lasting tribute to God's grace and prepares the way for a much greater display of grace than even Abraham could have possibly imagined.

In that same vicinity many, many years later, another "Only Son" would climb a nearby hill called Calvary or Golgotha. He too would carry the wood on His back. When at last He came to the appointed place, He was nailed to that cross and as He had earlier warned His disciples, He was lifted up to hang there and to die as the true Lamb of God, the promised substitute not only for Isaac, but for all the seed of Abraham, the seed of the woman. For Him, there was no last moment intervention nor a voice from heaven saying, "Do Him no harm" but only the mocking slander of His enemies and at last a heart-broken cry from His own lips, "My God, My God why have You forsaken Me?" Those haunting words from Psalm 22 were written by David in a time of uncertainty and grief, but they became almost the final prayer of Jesus before He died on that cross. But they were not the final words spoken, nor would they be His final prayer. For after these heart- broken words, Jesus would speak twice again saying "It is finished" and at the very end He dismissed His spirit into the Father's care, saying; "Father into Your hands I commit My spirit." Take courage, suffering saints, because of what Jesus accomplished on the cross, your last words too may be; "Father into Your hands I commit my spirit."

3

Killing of the Lamb

It was not difficult for the disciples of Jesus to believe that He had died. Of the 12 John at least was there when Jesus expired, and some of the women were there, too, and witnessed His death. Perhaps others of His disciples had seen what happened to Him from afar. But they all knew Jesus was dead, and this sad word quickly spread among many of His followers. Certainly Joseph of Arimathea, who was a secret disciple of Jesus, knew He was dead; for it was he, along with Nicodemus, another secret disciple, who had taken His body down from the cross with the permission of Pilate, the Roman governor. Together they had hastily prepared His body for interment and had placed that dear body in Joseph's own newly-hewn tomb. Oh yes, He was certainly dead. Upon investigation Pilate had certified His death, and he had even given permission to the Jewish authorities to place an official death seal on the tomb where He had been interred.

Then on the third day following His death and burial, some very strange and hard-to-believe rumors began to circulate that He was alive again. Certain of the women who had come to the tomb early Sunday morning with their spices and ointments intending to complete the embalmment of His body, said they had found the tomb empty. They also said angelic beings had told them that

He had actually risen from the dead, and these grieving women rushed to find Simon Peter and John to tell them what they had seen and heard. One of the women, Mary from Magdala, claimed that as she wept, Jesus Himself had appeared to her, called her by name, and commanded her to report to His "brothers" that he was truly alive again. Upon hearing the report from these women, Peter and John rushed to the tomb and found it empty. They left dismayed and confused because they had yet to understand the Scriptures that He must rise again from the dead. Apparently most of the disciples came together for mutual comfort and also to hide from the Jewish authorities, who would most certainly be looking for these men to punish them for their association with Jesus of Nazareth. The only exception was Judas who had committed suicide in remorse over his betrayal of Jesus.

Meanwhile two of Jesus' followers had left Jerusalem to return home to their village, Emmaus, seven miles out of Jerusalem. On that long road they had an unexpected encounter with a stranger to whom they poured out their tale of woe and grief about the death of Jesus. As it developed, that stranger was the Lord Himself who explained to them that His death and resurrection were the fulfillment of all that had been written in the Scriptures of the Old Testament. They hurried back to Jerusalem that very evening to share the wondrous encounter with the others. But before they could tell their glorious story, the 11 disciples and others gathered with them said that the Lord had arisen and had appeared to Simon Peter. "Then they told what had happened on the road and how He was known to them in the breaking of bread."

While they were all talking about these things, Jesus was suddenly there among them, giving the old familiar greeting "Shalom", which means "peace be with you." Their immediate reaction was doubt and fear. They thought that they had seen a ghost: (Which was exactly what they thought a year before when they saw Jesus walking towards them on the storm tossed sea.) Then Jesus said "Why are you troubled and why do doubts arise in your hearts? See My hands and feet that it is I, myself; touch me and see, for a spirit does not have flesh and bones as you see that I have". They still had doubts and they still did not believe that it was really Jesus. They seemed afraid to give in to their own joy, so Jesus said; "Have you anything here to eat?" They gave Him a piece of broiled fish, and He ate it in their sight. They were still unsure and perplexed, so Jesus opened their minds and hearts to understand the Scripture. He said to them, "These are My words which I spoke to you while I was still with you, that all things which are written about Me in the Law of Moses and the Prophets and the Psalms must be fulfilled." As their minds were opened to what Jesus was telling them, the whole of the Old Testament suddenly came into focus and that focus was Jesus Himself. Though they had doubted their own senses, when they realized that everything that happened to Jesus was according to God's plan from of old; then everything, even His death on the cross, fell into place; and they believed and they rejoiced.

The killing of Jesus of Nazareth, though a terrible miscarriage of justice, was the fulfillment of God's plan from the very beginning. This plan was revealed in the whole of the Old Testament, from Genesis through Malachi. How are we to understand this, and how does this help us to see the scope of God's magnificent plan? Neither time nor space nor your attention span allow for a complete explanation of how the killing of Jesus was foreseen in the entire Old Testament. Therefore, our attention will be focused on just a few particulars which will enable us to understand what Jesus helped His disciples understand on that Sunday evening so long ago. However, it needs to be said that the truth to which Jesus pointed His hopeful but doubtful disciples is an amazing testimony to the full inspiration and authenticity of the entire Bible. When seen through the eyes of the risen Jesus, everything written from Genesis 1:1 through Revelation 22:21 is inspired of God; and is truth itself. What we have in this sacred volume is a complete, reliable and trustworthy account of God's glorious plan of the ages to bring many sons and daughters to glory. What are these particulars which explain to us the reason and the need for the suffering and death of Jesus?

THE LAW OF MOSES.

It would be impossible in one book, much less one chapter of a book, to point to the many ways in which the eventual death of Jesus was pre-figured in the writings of Moses. The two great and inescapable analogies are seen in the story of the Passover and in the many sacrifices required to make atonement for the sins of God's people and to keep them in proper relationship with Him.

The story of the Passover needs to be very briefly recounted. The people of Israel had been in bitter bondage in Egypt for 400 years! Then God raised up a leader and a deliverer in the person of Moses. God had providentially prepared this man in many ways and then called him to this impossible task. Moses, at God's command, went to the Pharaoh of mighty Egypt and demanded that he release the Hebrew slaves. Of course, Pharaoh refused Moses' demand and began to increase his own demands on his slaves. He totally rejected God's word and mocked His messenger Moses.

At that point, Moses, at God's command, confronted stubborn Pharaoh with a request and a warning of dire consequences if he refused to obey the word of the Lord, to let His people go. Once more Pharaoh refused and began to oppress the enslaved Hebrews even more brutally than before. In the words of Scripture, repeated over and over again in the contest between Pharaoh's will and God's will: "But Pharaoh hardened his heart." Even after God began to send the devastating judgments on Pharaoh and upon the whole of Egypt, still he hardened his heart and would not obey the command of God to release the people of Israel. Every time one of these terrible plagues would fall on Egypt, Pharaoh would cry out and profess to repent of his stubborn unbelief; but as soon as the heavy hand of judgment was lifted, once more Pharaoh hardened his heart. Then the inevitable happened, and this presents a very serious warning to all. The hand of judgment upon Pharaoh took a new turn. By continually hardening his heart against God, Pharaoh opened himself to these dreadful words, "But the Lord hardened Pharaoh's heart." The hardening of one's heart to the Lord and His word will have the same dreadful consequence even to this very day.

There had been nine terrible plagues on Egypt and its people. There had been plagues of the river Nile and all the waters of Egypt turning into blood, and the multitudes of dead fish and animal life resulting. Then came the plagues of frogs, insects, the death of cattle, outbreak of boils, crushing hail, clouds of locusts, and three days of complete darkness. Still mighty Pharaoh, ruler of the great empire of Egypt, hardened his heart and suffered the consequences of his stubborn refusal...a hardened heart. But there would be even more dire consequences. The last of the plagues of judgment would devastate the land of Egypt and Pharaoh personally. In this plague, God decreed that the firstborn in every household from the highest (Pharaoh's family) to the lowest (the lowest slave) and even the firstborn of all the cattle would die. The Angel of Death would pass through the land, and as a result, all the first born would die. The only exception would be the people of Israel, for whom the Lord provided a way of escape from this dreadful plague. How ironic. Years before Pharaoh had issued a decree that all male babies of the Hebrews must be thrown into the river Nile. There seems to have been two motives behind this awful edict. First there was the growing concern over what seems to have been a population explosion among the Hebrew slaves which threatened the stability of the Empire. Second, of the many gods worshiped by the Egyptians the River Nile was prominent; and the crocodiles which inhabited that river were also worshiped. So what better way to appease the gods of the river than by offering them an unending supply of food?

However, for the people of Israel a way of escape was provided. For all who accepted God's provision, the Death Angel would pass over their homes and their firstborn would be spared (Thus the name Passover). Furthermore the people of Israel would not only be permitted to leave, they would be driven out of Egypt, never again to return to bondage and death. What form this Death Angel took, or what means it employed to do this deadly work, we are not told. What we are told is that this would be God's judgment upon Pharaoh and his people and at the same time His way of delivering His people, Israel, from this terrible judgment. God Himself would provide the means whereby His people would escape death and gain freedom. What was this provision and how does it help us to understand the killing of Jesus of Nazareth?

In the Passover celebration that God gave Moses to pass on to the people of Israel, detailed instructions were given to be followed carefully lest they too would be overtaken by the Death Angel. Each family or groups of families were to take a young lamb which had no defects or blemishes, keep it for four days, presumably to make sure no blemishes were observable. Then at evening on the fourth day, kill the lamb and roast it for eating. Along with unleavened bread and bitter herbs they were to consume it utterly, leaving no remnant of it until morning. The blood of the slain lamb was to be preserved and used to mark each house in which the Israelites lived. This was an external sign that those within the household were God's people under His protection. But why use blood for this designation? In the Old Testament there is always a connection between blood and life. The symbolism is obvious. The cost of redemption is death. The directions were sure and complete, and the promise secure, that in obeying the words of God they would be protected by His grace and power from the Angel of Death. By this the people would understand at least two things: the wages of sin is death, and only God can forgive sin and that at the cost of an innocent life. (The Passover lamb itself was only a symbol which would be fulfilled when Jesus became the true "Lamb of God who takes away the sin of the world). Before the lamb was killed there was, no doubt, explanation given as to the meaning of this sacrifice. Symbolically the sins of the people of Israel were transferred to the lamb; and when the innocent lamb was killed it was as a substitute for the people who deserved death. Again symbolically, when the lamb was killed, the people died also, and the price of sin (see Genesis 2:17) was paid.

Long, long after Moses taught the people of Israel these things, Jesus and His disciples faithfully followed all these instructions and had observed the Passover. As that feast drew towards an end, Jesus took a cake of unleavened bread and after blessing it, broke it in their presence saying; "Take, eat; this is my body." Then He took a cup, and after giving thanks, He gave it to them saying, "Drink from it all of you; for this is My blood of the covenant which is to be shed on behalf of many for forgiveness of sin." Then He added these words: "I will not drink of this fruit of the vine from now on until I drink it new with you in My Father's kingdom." By His words and deeds Jesus was demonstrating and fulfilling the true meaning of the Passover. If that is true, why did Jesus not take a piece of the Passover lamb and give it to His disciples? The Passover celebration required continual slaying of a lamb every year it was observed. What Jesus was saying, in effect, was that He was the true Lamb of God who takes away the sin of the world by His once-and-for all sacrifice. There would never again be the necessity of a symbolic sacrificial lamb for this would be fulfilled in His sacrifice on the cross. The disciples, and all who follow in their train, are given bread and the fruit of the vine as they celebrate the Passover of the New Covenant. They know that by His death their sins are forgiven. By His abiding presence they are sustained until that day when He shall gather to Himself all those for whom He died. Then He will, with them, celebrate the glorious conclusion of His life, death, resurrection, and ascension to the throne of the universe.

In the "Law of Moses" the whole complicated system of sacrifices foretold the death of Jesus and explained its meaning and its necessity. What were these many sacrifices, and in what sense was the death of Jesus the fulfillment of their meaning? The best answer to these questions is to be found in a commentary on the book of Leviticus by Professor John D. Currid, published by Evangelical Press, Darlington, England. In one of his introductory chapters, Leviticus and the New Testament, Professor Currid writes: "The sacrificial system of the Old Testament has ceased for the people of God." It has been fulfilled in the coming of Christ. We no longer need sacrifices because Christ offered Himself once and for all for the sins of His people. (Hebrews 10:8-14). A High Priest is not needed because Jesus Christ serves in that role. (Hebrews 4:14.) We do not need a tabernacle or a temple in which sacrifices take place because 'The Lord God, the Almighty, and the Lamb are the temple (Revelation 21:22). Christ's work on the cross, His

54

resurrection and ascension have made all these practices unnecessary. Yet it is important that the people of God today study the sacrificial laws in Leviticus because they are shadows and pointers to the work of Christ. By reading Leviticus one realizes the depth and pervasiveness of sin, the chasm between God and man and the absolute necessity of atonement to make mankind right with God. While the sacrificial system demonstrates these things, it also manifests its own insufficiency to meet these needs. Indeed it point so something greater to come and that is the fulfillment of the sacrificial system in the person and work of Jesus Christ. Sacrifice is thus to be considered applicable in a spiritual way to the Christian life. Yet this does not deny that the physical element of sacrifice also applies to the New Testament believer...Indeed for the believer to become a living sacrifice is the goal of the sacrificial ideal that began in the sacrificial worship of Leviticus. In other words, the literal performance of the sacrificial ritual ceased, yet the goal and the essence of the sacrifice, the priests and the sanctuary find their fulfillment in Christ and His believers."

THE PSALMS.

It may seem strange to realize that when the risen Jesus pointed His disciples to the Law of Moses and all the Prophets as proof that both His death and resurrection were according to God's plan and purpose, He also included the Psalms. That Jesus meant the whole Old Testament bore witness to Him there can be no doubt. However, since He mentioned the Psalms, it is important to look at a few specific references in the book of Psalms to see how they testify of Him and especially his death (and resurrection). Scattered throughout the book of Psalms there are quite a few of these inspired songs which are recognized as "Messianic Psalms" or songs which refer to the anticipated Messiah. Some of these are clearly Messianic in that they can only refer to the coming Messiah.

55

Others are Psalms with immediate reference to David the king, but are even more applicable to his holy descendant, the Messiah. For our purposes we will look at those Psalms which refer primarily to Christ's death and resurrection. Psalms 22 and 69 are the most explicit in describing the suffering and death of Jesus. Psalm 22 is quite graphic in describing His suffering and death. It is ironic that both Jesus and His enemies quoted from this Psalm as he was being crucified. As Jesus reached the terrible depths of his suffering and pain in body and spirit, he cried out to God in these words from Psalm 22: "My God, My God, why have you forsaken me?" His persecutors quoted from this Psalm in an entirely different spirit, by mocking Him with these words: "he trusted in God that he would deliver him, let Him deliver him if He delights in him." Verses 14-18 can only refer to Jesus' suffering on the cross. "I am poured out like water, all my bones are out of joint...my tongue sticks to my jaws...a company of evildoers encircles me...They have pierced my hands and my feet... they divide my garments among them, and for my clothing they cast lots."

Other Messianic Psalms are quoted in the New Testament as applying to Jesus before and after His resurrection and ascension. The truly great sermon preached by Simon Peter on the day of Pentecost relied heavily on two of these Psalms, 69 and 110, to explain both the suffering of Jesus and His triumph. A full discussion of the testimony of the book of Psalms is beyond the scope of this book.

ALL THE PROPHETS.
Jesus also told His disciples that all the Prophets spoke of His death and resurrection. Of all these Prophets, the one who wrote clearly and fully about these things was the Prophet Isaiah, who wrote eight centuries before the coming of Jesus Christ into the world. Isaiah's ministry covered a period of 50 years. According to

authentic Jewish tradition, he was of royal blood, being the grandson of the Jewish king Joash, and thus also a first cousin of king Uzziah, the longest reigning king in the history of Judah. Isaiah was a prolific writer who not only wrote the book that bears his name but also at least two other books mentioned in 2 Chronicles. One of these was a biography of king Uzziah, and the other was a record of the kings of Israel and Judah.

Isaiah is far better known for his signature work, the book of Isaiah. Truly he was the "Prince of the Prophets." He was quoted by the New Testament writers more than any other of the Old Testament prophets. The first place this occurs is found in Luke chapter 1 as well as Matthew 1. In these two places in which the conception and birth of Jesus is mentioned, these events are seen as a fulfillment of Isaiah's amazing prophecy that the Messiah will be Spirit conceived and Virgin born. Most of his Messianic passages have to do with the distant future and the glorious kingdom the Messiah will bring. Isaiah looked beyond his own time, and indeed beyond time itself, when he wrote of the eternal kingdom and the new (renewed) creation, the new heavens and earth. Isaiah saw the time coming when the Gentiles would be brought into the kingdom of God on equal footing with Israel. He also foretold that death itself would be destroyed and that there would be a glorious resurrection for God's people. It is worth noting that Jesus not only quoted Isaiah, but that all of His preaching and teaching was very similar to that of Isaiah and was in agreement with him. When John the Baptist was in prison for his courageous rebuke of Herod's immorality, he sent word by his disciples to ask Jesus if he was indeed the coming Messiah, or would another come. This is not the place to work through all the dynamics of this incident, but the answer Jesus sent to John was that He, Jesus, was fulfilling the messianic role as foreseen by Isaiah in Isaiah 35, and 61.

Perhaps the most amazing of all his prophecy is found in Isaiah 53. In this chapter his focus is on the suffering of the Messiah, and the account of His suffering is almost more graphic than the actual account of His crucifixion described in the four Gospels. When the risen Jesus Christ talked with His disciples on that joyful evening of long ago, they seemed unable to believe that he was really alive again. They thought they were seeing a ghost and were unable to trust even their own senses, or even to believe what they saw and heard. However, when Jesus opened their understanding to the Scriptures of the Old Testament the truth and meaning of His death and resurrection became clear; and from that point on they became what he had called them to be, world changers. I think the key passage to which he pointed them had to be Isaiah 53.

Early in His ministry Jesus began to tell the disciples that He must suffer many things and be killed by crucifixion. These brave young men refused to believe this could possibly happen to Him, for they were sure He was the promised Messiah. They were so focused on the prophecies of His glorious victory and reign they could not comprehend His warnings about the coming inevitable suffering and death that awaited Him. This simply did not fit in with what they believed and what they had been taught to expect when Messiah came. If they considered Isaiah 53 at all, they probably thought that this applied only to what the nation of Israel had already suffered at the hands of her conquering enemies down through her long history. This seems to have been the wide spread belief of many in Israel at that time. It is also the interpretation of many to this day who reject Jesus Christ as the Messiah.

But now they had witnessed for themselves the things Jesus had warned them about. They could no longer deny the truth he had so often tried to teach them during His earthly ministry. He had suffered many things. He had been betrayed into the hands of sinful men, and had been condemned to die. The religious leaders had persuaded the Romans to confirm his death penalty and to crucify Him. They had seen Him die and they had seen his body buried. Even as they had refused to believe Him when he told them he must die, so they did not understand him when he also added, "and be raised again on the third day". What Jesus was doing in that upper room on that Sunday evening was to put it all together for them. If indeed He was opening their minds to understand Isaiah 53, what better way to enable them to see how His death and resurrection were part of the master plan from the very beginning. Since this chapter from the prophet Isaiah is so crucial to understanding that the suffering and death of Jesus, followed by His resurrection, were indeed at the very heart of God's eternal plan, the following chapter in this book will be devoted to a more careful study of Isaiah 53.

4

Incredible Prophecy in Isaiah 53

Of all the Prophets of the Old Testament who foretold of the coming Messiah, Isaiah was truly the "Prince of the Prophets." In the introduction to his most excellent commentary on the book of Isaiah, Professor Allan Harmon makes the following observation. "The number of quotations from and allusions to Isaiah that appear in the New Testament is striking. Approximately one third of the New Testament is made up of direct quotations or indirect allusions to the Old Testament, and of the Old Testament books the Psalms and Isaiah are those drawn upon most often. About twenty times Isaiah is cited by name...Of Isaiah 53, all but one verse is quoted in the New Testament...Jesus' own public ministry began with a sermon on Isaiah 61 in which he made this declaration: 'Today this scripture has been fulfilled in your hearing.'"

The amazing message of Isaiah 53 which pictures so graphically the suffering of the Savior really begins in Isaiah 52:13 with these contrasting words concerning God's servant (Jesus of Nazareth): "Behold My servant will prosper. He will be high and lifted up, and greatly exalted...His appearance was marred more than any man and His form more than the sons of men." Following these mysterious words the lament recorded in Isaiah 53 begins. Some have attempted to say that this is a reference to the nation of Israel. Yet before the Christian era the Jewish scholars were almost universal in agreeing this applied to the coming Messiah. Some of their manuscripts actually inserted the word Messiah when mention was made of "my servant".

The first paragraph of this chapter sets the tone for all that follows. The question is pondered by the Prophet when he asks: "Who has believed our message? To whom has the arm of the Lord been revealed?" Most certainly these questions applied to the experience of Jesus of Nazareth in His earthly ministry. Though at times He was eagerly heard by many, yet as His message became widely spread throughout Galilee and Judea, there were relatively few who believed in Him or who accepted His teaching.

Following the prophet's two questions there follows a description of the humility of the coming Messiah. He was not to appear in a cloud of great glory (not yet!), but rather in the form of a "tender shoot like a root growing out of dry ground." One of the reasons why Jesus was not accepted by the great majority of his contemporaries was they were looking for a great warrior King who would bring punishment and death upon the enemies of Israel. Many of the Galileans knew Him only as the son of Mary and Joseph, a humble carpenter. So when Jesus preached in the Synagogue that he was the long awaited Messiah, they reacted with scorn and hostility. "Who does He think He is? We know where he comes from and we know all His family. When the true Messiah comes, we will not know where He is from." They were unconsciously fulfilling Isaiah's prophetic lament, "He has no stately form or majesty that we should look to Him, nor appearance that we should be attracted to Him."

Hostile indifference would quickly become adamant rejection and aggressive condemnation. The Prophet continued in his lament by saying "He is despised and rejected by men." That prophecy would be fulfilled in the life and ministry of Jesus of Nazareth. Early in his public ministry Jesus went into the synagogue at Nazareth where He was brought up and was handed the book of Isaiah to read. He opened the scroll to Isaiah 61 and began to read. "The Spirit of the Lord God is upon me; because of this He has anointed me to proclaim good news to the poor. He has sent me to proclaim liberty to the captives and recovering of sight to the blind, to set at liberty those who are oppressed, to proclaim the year of the Lord's favor." Jesus said to the assembled congregation, "Today this Scripture has been fulfilled in your hearing." He went on to expound on this passage and make application which offended the people to the point they drove Him out of the Synagogue and out of the city. They even tried to kill Him by throwing Him over the cliff. But He passed through their midst and left Nazareth.

Truly the hostility towards Him had quickly turned into rejection and condemnation. So not only was Isaiah 61 fulfilled, but also Isaiah 53:3. This would become a pattern in His ministry. Because of His many miracles of healing and mercy, He was at first accepted and applauded, but when He proclaimed the word of God, the message and the messenger were rejected. He was indeed a man of sorrows and acquainted with grief. His suffering and sorrow would come to painful end when He was crucified. But even before this, He would experience the burden of being reviled and rejected by His own people. He had to endure the rejection of His claims by His own family members. His brothers taunted Him to go to Jerusalem and make His claims there. At one point, even His mother Mary and His siblings came to Him and wanted to take Him back to their home. They thought He Was beside Himself, and were embarrassed by Him and for Him. Mary, His mother, seemed to forget what had been told her by God's angel about her coming Son.

The leaders of the religious establishment, who should have been the first to welcome Him and proclaim the good news, became His most bitter and implacable foes. From the very beginning of His ministry, they despised and rejected Him. This was only the beginning of His sorrows and grief. At the very end, even His closest friends and disciples forsook Him and fled away; leaving Him alone in the hands of His bitter enemies. Of that small core group of twelve men, His close friends, one would betray Him, one would deny Him, and the rest would flee from Him.

When Jesus was brought to trial before the ruling Sanhedrin, no one stood up for Him. Even though there must have been some present at that trial who had been deeply impressed by His miracles and His messages none had the courage to defend Him. One of the most respected members of the ruling class, Nicodemus, had come to Him by night and said, "Rabbi, we know that you are a teacher sent from God; for no one can do these do these miraculous signs which you are doing except God be with him." Was Nicodemus present when Jesus was placed on trial for His life? Or had he knowingly absented himself not wanting to be a part of His condemnation? By their silence, those who may have believed He was at least a good man and a messenger sent from God joined in despising and rejecting Him. Maybe this guilty silence is what the prophet had in mind when he said, "And we hid, as it were, our faces from Him; He was despised we did not esteem Him."

As Isaiah's lament continues and deepens in pathos, it becomes clear that the Servant of the Lord is not suffering for any wrong doing on His part, but for others. Notice the contrast between the personal pronouns. He has borne our griefs; and He has carried our sorrows. Yet when this prophecy was fulfilled in the life and death of Jesus of Nazareth did anyone consider this? All who saw

Him suffer saw this as a sign of God's disapproval of Him. They even mocked His dying pain and sorrow by railing at Him as He hung on the cross. "He trusted in God that he would deliver Him. Let Him deliver Him if He delights in Him." Not only did He suffer for us, but His suffering resulted in our benefit and blessing. Once again the contrast in personal pronouns tells the story. "He was wounded (to death) for our Transgressions. He was crushed for our iniquities. The Chastisement for our peace was upon Him. By His deep wounds, we are healed."

That His suffering was vicarious is further emphasized by the prophet's confession for himself and for us, "All we like sheep have gone astray; we have turned, every one of us, to his own way. And the Lord has laid on Him the iniquity of us all." Our relief, our healing, our exoneration were all at the cost of His extreme suffering and death.

Though He was entirely guiltless and His suffering was all in behalf of others, He did not complain or even speak up for Himself. "He was oppressed and afflicted, yet He opened not His mouth." (In fear and exasperation, Pilate had shouted at Jesus, "Speak up man, don't you hear what they are charging you with? Tell me, who are you, where are you from. Answer me! I have the authority to release you or to crucify You!" To which Jesus only answered, "You would have no authority over me at all, were it not given you from above.") "He was led as a lamb to the slaughter, and as a sheep is silent before its shearers, so He opened not His mouth."

After Jesus had been so unjustly condemned by the Sanhedrin, He was sent to the Roman authorities for the confirmation of the death penalty they demanded. So the words of Isaiah, "He was taken from prison and from judgment, and who shall declare His generation? For He was cut off from the land of the living." By these words it becomes abundantly clear that the suffering described by the prophet results in the death of the Servant. The words which follow, "For the transgressions of My people, was He stricken," emphasize again that His suffering and death were vicarious and not because He was guilty of any crime or sin. This truth becomes the foundation for the Gospel His disciples were to proclaim. It remains foundational forever.

After being judged and sentenced, He experienced what all but He deserve, death. They treated Him as if He was guilty, and made no plans for His burial. No doubt the thought occurred to His enemies, with gleeful satisfaction at the irony of it, "let us bury Him in the potter's field purchased by the money returned by His betrayer. But it was not to be. For a very rich and prominent man, Joseph of Arimathea, who was a secret admirer of Jesus, placed His body in the tomb prepared for himself. Thus was fulfilled the strange words of Isaiah, "But with the rich at His death, because he had done no violence, nor was any deceit in His mouth."

The following verses from the lament will form the basis on which Simon Peter would preach his famous Pentecost sermon which resulted in mass conversions to Jesus Christ just a few weeks later. "Yet it pleased the Lord to crush Him; He has put Him to grief." (Men of Israel, hear these words: Jesus of Nazareth a man attested by God to you by miracles, wonders and signs which God did through Him in your midst, as you yourselves know—Him being delivered by the determined counsel and foreknowledge of God, you have taken with lawless hands, have crucified and put to death.") The suffering experienced by God's Servant, and foretold by God's prophet are in fulfillment of His glorious plan of redemption. He who "made Him to be sin, who knew no sin," did so because He was also determined that those for whom the Servant would suffer, would become "the righteousness of God through Him." Isaiah had foreseen this when he said, "When You make His soul an offering for sin, He shall see His seed, he shall prolong His days, and the pleasure of the Lord will proper in His hand." He shall see the travail of His soul, and be satisfied. By His knowledge My righteous Servant shall justify many, for he shall bear their iniquities."

But by the inspiration of the Holy Spirit, the prophet also saw beyond the death of Jesus of Nazareth, and foresaw His glorious resurrection when he said; "Therefore I will divide the spoil with the strong, because He poured out His soul unto death, and He was numbered with the transgressors, and He bore the sins of many, and made intercession for the transgressors."

Therefore it is both pointless and wrong to attempt to tell the story of the killing of Jesus of Nazareth without also telling the rest of the story, His resurrection from the dead. What God has joined together, let no mere man ever, ever put asunder.

5

Birth and Early Years of Jesus of Nazareth

In fulfillment of prophecy and the plan of God, the long years of waiting were over and Jesus came into the world. It happened this way. Another birth preceded His. An elderly couple, a priest and his wife, were well past the normal years of child bearing, but they had a son. He was to become the fore runner and the herald of the coming Messiah. His name was John, and there is much about his early life of which we know next to nothing. He would have inherited the office of Priest, but as far as we know he never served in that capacity. He chose rather the life of a hermit in the wilderness and apparently understood his role as the herald of the coming Messiah. He was to be the predicted "Elijah" who would usher in the kingdom of God. Like Elijah of old, he lived in the wilderness and shunned the easier life of city and temple.

When he was thirty years of age, he began his ministry of preaching and calling upon the nation to repent of its sins and prepare for the Messiah whose kingdom was at hand. He obviously was a man with charisma and spiritual power, and his preaching reached the minds and hearts of multitudes. Many thought John was the promised Messiah, but he disclaimed that role. John required those who came to hear him and believed his preaching to be baptized as a symbol of repentance and cleansing. The whole nation was deeply stirred and thousands sought the baptism he preached. The Jewish historian Josephus testified that John's influence was wide spread and that even many of the leaders and rulers were deeply touched. His whole ministry centered around the proclamation that the Messiah's coming was at hand and that all the people must repent of their sins and prepare for the inauguration of His kingdom.

At the height of John's popularity and power, Jesus of Nazareth began his public ministry. When John saw Him approaching, he uttered these immortal words; "Behold the Lamb of God who takes away the sin of the world." He also added these words, "He must increase and I must decrease." Shortly thereafter John publicly anointed Jesus to begin His public ministry. In God's mysterious providence John indeed did decrease and was executed by Herod the Tetrarch because John had rebuked him for his adulterous affair with his brother's wife. So John disappeared from the scene shortly after Jesus began His public ministry. In designating Jesus as "The Lamb of God who takes away the sins of the world," John was prophesying the necessity of Jesus' death. In the Old Testament system of sacrifices, the "Lamb of God" was the Passover lamb which was killed, symbolically bearing the sins of the people. Now the true Lamb of God was at hand, and by his sacrificial death all sins of all God's people would be taken away, once and for all.

The birth of Jesus happened this way. The young virgin Mary was engaged to be married to a man named Joseph of Galilee, a carpenter by trade. The usual custom in that day and place was that a young girl would be betrothed to a man while she was in her teens, and this was a binding agreement which could only be broken by death or divorce. Both Joseph and Mary were descended from David the King, and the importance of this would soon be seen. During this interim time for Joseph and Mary, Mary had

a startling experience which threatened not only her future marriage, but her life as well. She was visited by a messenger from God,
the Angel Gabriel, who told her she was to be the mother of the
long expected Messiah. His exact words were, "Hail, you are rich-
ly blessed! The Lord is with you." Mary was greatly frightened by
this greeting and did not understand what it meant. So the Angel
continued: "Fear not, Mary, for you have found favor with God.
And you will conceive in your womb and bring forth a son; and
you shall call his name Jesus. He will be great, and will be called
the Son of the Highest. And the Lord God will give unto Him the
throne of His father David; He will reign over the house of Jacob
forever, and of His kingdom there shall be no end."

Mary's incredulous response to the Angel was "How can this be,
since I have known no intimacy with a man?" The Angel's answer
was "The Holy Spirit will come upon you, and the power of the
Highest will overshadow you; wherefore also the holy child born
of you will be called the Son of God." And Mary said "Behold I
am the bond servant of the Lord; let it be to me according to your
word." Who was this young woman Mary, and how could she have
such willing obedience to the message from God which could
threaten not only her happiness, but also her very life? (Not the
Mary of cult and legend, but the Mary of Scripture; the only Mary
we can authentically know.) What sort of woman was she? What is
the message of her life and faith for us today?

The great reformer Martin Luther said that Mary was a humble,
simple peasant girl going about her chores at home or else doing
daily devotionals when the angel came to her (which is a pretty
good guess). But Mary's incredible humility and faith are far beyond what might have been expected and is not a matter of speculation. The first mark of true greatness is always humility. Though

she was of royal blood, being a descendant of David, Mary possessed and exercised the quality of humility beyond mere greatness. We never find Mary attempting to glorify herself for the role God gave her in the earthly birth of His Son. Indeed the veneration and adoration heaped upon her through tradition and legend which rightly belong only to her Son must grieve her humble heart. Mary's response to the angelic announcement was a very humble one, "Behold the handmaid of the Lord."

Perhaps the very humility of God Himself becoming also a man played a part in Mary's humility. If God had so humbled himself by becoming a man, how could she be proud or haughty? Jesus said He was meek and lowly of heart—a quality He first saw in His mother.

Above all her other qualities, it is Mary's faith that shines the brightest. She well knew that the story of the Angel's visit and his incredible message to her would be rejected and ridiculed. She knew her integrity and purity would be questioned by all and especially her beloved Joseph. She knew that Joseph was well within his rights by the law of Moses to have her openly accused, convicted, and stoned to death. Yet by faith Mary accepted God's will for her life, and her death, if need be. God honored her faith and protected her. Her faith was greatly strengthened by her visit to her aged cousin, Elizabeth, who was also pregnant and that far beyond the years of child birth. Before Mary could tell the news to Elizabeth that she too was pregnant, and that in a supernatural way; Elizabeth greeted Mary as the mother of her Lord, and rejoiced with her.

Almost immediately after Mary gave birth to Jesus in a mean and lowly place, a cattle stall, some humble shepherds came looking for the holy infant for they too had been visited by angels who announced His birth. Much later after Joseph had found a place for his family somewhere in Bethlehem, some strange visitors showed up to pay homage and give worship to the child who in their words was "King of the Jews."

But what of Joseph, the man to whom Mary was engaged when it was discovered that she was "with child"? At first he was inclined to break the bonds of betrothal and had the option of public accusation. But Joseph, heart-broken Joseph, was not that sort of man. He had decided to take the option of privately breaking the engagement bonds. Because he was a just and merciful man he would not see Mary openly disgraced and punished. Since there is no record of Joseph's thoughts or words when he discovered Mary's condition, we are left with only our imagination to fill in the story of his pain and agony of spirit. No doubt he tried to think, but how does one think coherently when the heart is broken and the mind in a state of shock? No doubt he kept seeing her young beautiful and innocent face as she tried to tell him her news. "Innocent? O God of my fathers if only she were." Her words still echoed in his ears. He tried to remember all she had told him. An angel of the Lord had come to her, she said. She was chosen to bear the Messiah, she claimed. She was even now with child she admitted. He could hear nor remember no more. He sent her back to her parent's house and told her to wait until he could decide what to do with her. But while he was agonizing over these things, groaning and weeping before the Lord, he fell into a deep sleep of utter exhaustion. God would also comfort and strengthen Joseph as he had Mary. While in this deep sleep, Joseph had a dream. But it was more than just a dream! He also received a heavenly visitor. I like to think that this too was Gabriel, who had told Mary the great truth of her coming child. In the dream he heard a heavenly voice saying; "Joseph, son of David, do not fear to take Mary as your wife, for that which is conceived in her is from the Holy Spirit. She will bear this son and you shall call his name Jesus, for it is He who will save His people from their sins. All this is fulfillment of the prophetic words of old: 'Behold the virgin shall conceive and bear a son and they shall call his name Immanuel (which means God with us)."

Joseph's response to the angelic words was just like Mary's...obedient faith. For "when Joseph woke from his sleep he did just what the Angel of the Lord had commanded him: he took Mary as his wife, but did not know her intimately until after she had given birth to a son. And he called his name Jesus." While still in Bethlehem, Joseph and Mary took their young son to the temple to observe all the requirements of the law in His behalf. So on the eighth day of his life he received the mark of the covenant in his tiny body, circumcision. The law also required that forty days after the birth of a first born son an offering was to be made for the ceremonial purification of the mother and the presentation of the child to the Lord. This offering was in recognition that the first born son belonged to the Lord, but also that God accepted a substitute for the life of the child. Joseph and Mary brought the appropriate offering and also dedicated their son to the service of the Lord.

As they entered the temple for the ceremony, they were met by an elderly man, Simeon, devout and righteous, who was also Spirit filled. The Holy Spirit had revealed to him that he would not die until he had seen the Messiah with his own eyes. Guided by the Spirit he had come to the temple just as Joseph and Mary brought Jesus for the sacred rites prescribed by the law. As soon as he saw the baby, he knew this was the promised One. Filled with joy and awe, Simeon took baby Jesus in his arms blessing God and saying: "Now, O Lord, You are letting Your servant depart in peace, according to Your word! For my eyes have seen Your salvation which You have prepared in the presence of all peoples, a light for revelation to the Gentiles and glory to your people Israel."

74

Joseph and Mary were amazed at these words which were said concerning Jesus. Simeon blessed them and said to Mary, "This child is destined to cause the falling and rising of many in Israel and for a sign that is spoken against, (and a sword will pierce your heart also), that the thoughts of many hearts may be revealed." Mary had heard many wonderful things about her son before and after he was born, but was not prepared for these strange words from Simeon. Did the shadow of the cross fall upon her heart that day?

There was also an elderly widow, Anna, who was in the temple at the same time, for night and day she came before the Lord in prayer and fasting. She no doubt heard the words of Simeon, and the Lord opened her heart to believe that this tiny baby was indeed the Messiah. She gave praise to the Lord and spoke about Jesus to all who were looking for the coming Savior. I don't think this was just a momentary, passing comment. As long as the Lord continued to give her life and strength, she bore her wondering witness; for she had seen the Savior, the one of whom the prophets had spoken long before. Before long, two elderly saints would finish their course on earth and would, in the words of Simeon, depart this life in peace and enter into the joy of their Lord. That same glorious possibility awaits any who hear and believe their words.

What is omitted in Luke's birth narratives concerning Jesus is fully presented in Matthew's gospel. There we learn of the attempts of evil king Herod to find and destroy the One he was told who had been born King of the Jews. Herod, when he heard the report of the mysterious visitors from the east that a star had guided them to Jerusalem to seek and find the recently born King of the Jews, was filled with bitter anger and terror. He set out to find and destroy this latest threat to his throne and power. The "seed of the serpent" was determined to kill the "seed of the woman." It seemed so one sided at the time. How could a helpless little baby stand up to a wicked, and by this time insane, powerful ruler who even had the backing of the greatest Empire the world had ever seen? The contestants in this epic struggle were mighty Herod and a powerless, helpless baby.

They called him Herod the Great. He was a man of great power and authority. He was king over all Judea by the grace of the Roman Empire. In all the turmoil that had shaken that mighty empire, Herod had very slyly and skillfully played one coalition against another. At the time Jesus was born, he had managed to get into the good graces of Caesar Augustus and seemed secure in his position of power. Yet he ever lived in a state of paranoia and fear. He was also a very sick man in every way and probably had little more than a year to live. He knew the Jews feared and hated him because he was not a Jew by birth, but an Edomite. They also knew his confessed conversion to Judaism was not sincere, but only a political ploy to remain in power. He would stop at nothing to keep his position and his power. He had arranged the assassination of the high priest who had opposed him. Thousands of prominent Jewish leaders had also been executed on the pretext they too had plotted against him. Knowing of the wide- spread rejection and hatred of him, Herod made a decree that on the day of his death, the head of every household in Judea was to be killed. If they (the Jews) would not mourn him, they would at least mourn. Fortunately this decree was not carried out, but that he made such a decree is indicative of the state of his mind and madness.

He was also aware that the prophets had said a descendant of David would one day occupy the position he now had and clung to so fervently. So determined was he to hold on to his throne that he had three of his own sons murdered lest they lay claim to that seat of power. One of his ten wives, who had been his favorite, was involved in plots against him, or so he thought, so she too must die. By his orders, Mariamne was strangled; and later even her mother Alexandra was also executed.

That was Herod the Great. Who dared oppose him or present a threat to his rule? So when he heard a report that visitors from the east, the Magi, were seeking the one who was born King of the Jews, he was troubled, fearful and angry. When great Herod was troubled, all Jerusalem trembled too; for all knew of his madness and his authority to destroy anyone who might be a threat. He called together the scholars of the Jews and demanded to know where this interloper would be born according to the prophets of old. He was told that the long awaited Messiah, the King of the Jews, would be born in Bethlehem of Judea according to the prophet Micah. He must find and kill this usurper, whoever he might be. After interviewing the Magi, Herod professed a desire to find and worship this "King of the Jews" whom they were seeking. So he sent them to Bethlehem with the specific orders to find him and bring him word of their discovery. He sent them on this mission with these orders, "Go and search diligently for the child, and when you have found him bring me word, that I too may come and worship him." Of course, Herod's true intention was to find the child, identify him, and have him murdered.

Following the star that led them to Judea in their search for the king of the Jews, the Magi came to the village of Bethlehem. They had probably traveled a thousand miles to reach Jerusalem. They were now only a little over 10 miles from their ultimate destination, Bethlehem. The luminary they had followed so far now turned south and led them not only to Bethlehem, but to the very house where Joseph had brought his little family. It is not the purpose of this book to discuss the details of the Magi, who they were or from where they had come, but a few things need to be said about them and their seeking journey. As best we know these men came from the former Persian Empire. That they were influenced by the large Jewish population of that area is obvious. That they were influenced by the writings of Daniel and other Jewish prophets is most probable. Daniel was a captive of the Babylonian Army when they conquered Judah and sacked Jerusalem. He was among the favored few who were trained in Babylonian lore and learning and prepared for government services. He was highly valued and promoted to a place of prominence in Babylon. Later when the Persians overthrew Babylon and initiated a new Empire, Daniel was selected to serve the new rulers and was highly thought of. His influence even over the kings was amazing. He survived at least one attempt to assassinate him and probably several such assaults in his long life. He was in a unique position to influence the course of events in that powerful empire, and his most significant writings are preserved to this very day. All of this is to say it is very plausible to assume the Magi, the scholars and inheritors of the wisdom of long history, were greatly influenced by this remarkable man from another era. Certainly there were references in Daniel's writings to the future mighty king who would come at the appointed time and place.

When the Magi arrived in Bethlehem, they came to the house where Joseph had brought his family. It must have been startling to him and to Mary to see these lordly men cast themselves down on their faces and worship their infant Son. Next they opened their treasure-chests and gave Him gifts of gold, frankincense and myrrh. One of the early church fathers, Origen, said of these gifts, "gold as to a king; myrrh as to a mortal man, and frankincense as to God." These gifts from these men were intended to show their honor to and faith in this little child as being more than mere man.

Meanwhile back in Jerusalem, Herod was anxiously waiting for their return so he could end this threat to his throne. Two dreams and obedient response to those dreams frustrated the evil plans of Herod. First the Magi (or wise men as we have called them) had a dream in which they were warned that Herod's purpose was murder, not worship. Thus they left for their own country by another way. Meanwhile Joseph, who had already been instructed by God in a dream, had another dream in which God's angel warned him to take the child and his mother immediately and to flee into Egypt, beyond the reach of Herod. That very night he took Mary and Jesus and fled into Egypt. Their travel and stay in Egypt was probably financed by the treasures the Magi had given to Jesus.

When anxious, fearful Herod realized that he had been tricked by the Magi, his rage and fury knew no end. He immediately ordered a squad of soldiers to rush to Bethlehem and kill all male babies from two years old and younger, and that grisly deed was carried out immediately. Selfish ambition driven to the extreme always tends to produce cruelty and death to any who would pose a threat to that ambition. That pattern has been reproduced down through the ages and into our own time. This terrible mandate of Herod would be among the last decrees he would ever issue, for shortly after this he would die. As the Scripture tells us, "It is appointed unto man once to die and after this the judgment." The judgment which awaited Herod is beyond our knowledge and even our imagination.

Herod was thwarted in his effort to kill Jesus. From all appearance he was all powerful, and the infant Jesus so helpless and powerless. But outward appearances are not the whole story. Who is this whom Herod fears so greatly? Surely He was more than the infant son of peasant parents. How could a tiny baby boy living in poverty with no one to defend him except a very young mother and a hard working but poor foster father pose a threat to such power Herod held? When Joseph was warned by God in a dream to flee into Egypt with Mother and child, he did the only thing he could do to save his family, he fled. There was nothing he could have done to prevent the slaughter that followed his flight. Probably in his simple honesty he could not have imagined what Herod would do; or having imagined it, could not have prevented it. But if what the angel of God had told both Mary and Joseph about this child was true, Herod had every right to be troubled and fearful. Gabriel told Mary (and later Joseph) that Jesus would inherit the throne of David and reign over the house of Jacob forever, and of His kingdom there would be no end. If this coming One was the fulfillment of prophecy, He was not only the everlasting king, he was also the wonderful counselor, the mighty God, the everlasting Father, the prince of peace. In one of the messianic psalms we discover that He was destined to destroy all earthly powers who opposed Him and bring all nations under His reign.

Much later, when Jesus was on trial for His life before the Roman governor, Pontius Pilate, Pilate asked of Him, "Are you a King". When Jesus answered him, "My kingdom is not of this world," Pilate concluded that Jesus was no threat to the Roman Empire or to the Emperor. Pilate was wrong! This was a promise and a warning that beyond all earthly powers, His kingdom was an everlasting kingdom which would at last prevail over all and never end.

When Herod ordered the execution of all the male babies in and around Bethlehem, he thought he had ended the threat of this potential usurper, and that his power and kingdom were safe again. Little did he know that this helpless baby would outlive him by thirty years, and that in the very end, to Him every knee would bow and every tongue confess that He was Lord of all.

The outcome of this contest? Listen to these words: "Now when Herod was dead, and angel of the Lord appeared unto Joseph in Egypt, saying, 'arise and go into the land of Israel; for they are dead who sought the young child's life." Who would have thought that this tiny baby boy would survive Herod and his mad attempt at murder? In the heat of the battle who would have thought that Jesus would live and Herod would die? There is something of the warning of doom found in these words, "they are dead who sought the young child's life." The conflict is ongoing. The story does not end with the above words. There would continue to be many "Herods" down through the long course of history. You know the names of some at least: Pilate, Caesar, Nero, Tamer the Lame, Attila, Napoleon, Hitler, Stalin, and many others. The roll call of the tyrants is almost unending. These "Herods" and countless others have brought unimaginable suffering, sorrow and horror upon helpless victims of their ambition and wrath. Herod's cruelty and record of murders is dwarfed by many others, and still the story goes on and on and will continue until at last final justice is brought to pass by Him before whom all must appear in Judgment. Yes Herod is dead, but Jesus lives! Why? Because another death awaits Jesus just a few short years later. That awaiting death will be much more terrible than a sudden stab or slash by one of Herod's hired assassins. But the story of that awful death must await a later chapter.

The only other information we have of the early life of Jesus is found in the Gospel of Luke. In this brief account of Jesus going to the temple in Jerusalem at the age of twelve, we are given one glimpse of Jesus' awareness of the meaning of His life and mission even at this tender age. This was the approximate age at which a young Jewish boy would declare himself to be a Bar Mitzvah (a son of the law). But whether Jesus assumed the formal responsibilities of being a law keeper at this time we do not know, but what we are told points to Jesus' awareness of why He had been sent into the world. Apparently a large number of people from Galilee had come for the festivities associated with the observance of the Passover, and this may account for the confusion which resulted in Jesus being left behind. After a frantic search by Joseph and Mary, Jesus was found in the temple seated in the midst of the rabbis listening and asking questions. To the amazement of these learned men, Jesus answered their questions with deep insight into the Word of God. Mary's understandable anxiety is expressed in these words; "Child why have you dealt thus with us? In anguish your father and I have been seeking you."

Jesus' reply tells us much about His awareness and commitment to doing what he had been sent into the world to accomplish. Mary had used the expression, "your father and I." Jesus responded, "Why have you been seeking me? Did you not know that I must be in my Father's house?" As Hendricksen says in his commentary, "Note the contrast, 'your father', my Father. The contrast tells the whole story." The expression, "I must" is used over and over again by Jesus. The driving force of his life was to do the will of Him who sent him into the world. At one point it was said of Jesus that "He must go through Samaria." Why? Because He was seeking the lost there in that village of Sychar. Shortly before His arrest, trial and death Jesus had said to His disciples, "I must go to Jerusalem and be betrayed into the hands of sinners, and suffer many things, and be crucified." His ambition and determination was to do the will of the Father even though this would mean unspeakable suffering on His part, including being made a sacrifice on the cross for the sins of His people. Yes, even at this young and tender age, Jesus knew why He had been sent into the world. He knew He must die to fulfill His destiny.

Rising Tide of Rejection and Deadly Hostility

When Jesus was little more than an infant, probably no more than two years old, King Herod tried his best to kill Him. When He began His public ministry, He would face a rising tide of rejection and deadly hostility.

There is no record of the life of Jesus between the time, when at the age of twelve, He went to Jerusalem with His parents; when, at the age of thirty, He began his public ministry. John the Baptist, Jesus' forerunner, emerged from the wilderness where he had grown up, and began to call God's people to repentance and faith. His preaching must have been powerful indeed, for large crowds from all over Judea and Galilee went out to hear him. His message was full of hope and promise. According to John, The long awaited Messiah was at hand. Therefore he called upon the people to prepare for this grand event by publicly submitting to water baptism as a sign of their repentance. This in itself was an amazing requirement, for up to this point, only Gentile converts to Judaism were required to submit to this symbolic "bath", confessing that they were unclean. Now, here was John, by implication, declaring that the Jews were also unclean and in need of baptism and the repentance this represented.

The religious establishment angrily rejected John's ministry, nor did they consent to his baptism. "The very idea!" they thought. "We are God's chosen people and clean because of the covenant God made with Abraham. What does this mad man think he is doing?" But it seems the "establishment" had lost touch with the people. Thousands responded to John's call, and received this baptism gladly. John also kept emphasizing that the Messiah and His kingdom were at hand. He was the mighty one who would baptize by the Holy Spirit and by fire. This was the good news that God's chosen people had longed for, prayed for and awaited for many centuries.

One day as John was proclaiming the good news of the approaching kingdom, he saw Jesus of Nazareth coming towards him. Suddenly he knew, by God's Spirit of revelation filling his heart, Jesus was the Messiah he had been proclaiming! Speaking by that same Spirit and His revelation, John pointed to Jesus as He drew near and said, "Behold the Lamb of God who takes away the sin of the world." John was obviously a student of the Old Testament. Now he was saying of Jesus, that He was the suffering servant who bore the sins of many, as foretold by Isaiah the prophet. For long years the people of Israel had longed and waited for the Messiah who would overcome the hated Romans, and restore the kingdom of David. Apparently the words of Isaiah and other prophets concerning the sufferings of the Messiah, had been conveniently set aside, or interpreted to mean the sufferings of Israel as a nation. For whatever reason, the people were not expecting the One who would be rejected, but One who would destroy the enemies of Israel and restore the throne of David.

Then an amazing thing happened. Jesus came to John and requested that he baptize Him. John would have refused Him, saying, "I have need to be baptized by You, and You are coming to me?" Jesus responded, "Grant that it be so now; for it is fitting, by this act, that we fulfill all righteousness."

How are we to understand this act of John in baptizing Jesus? What did it mean then, and what meaning does it have for us now? The most common answer, accepted by many, is that Jesus submitted to John's baptism as an example for us to follow. If that was the meaning, does it not seem odd that later on, as recorded in the book of Acts, the Apostle Paul required certain men, who had been baptized by John the Baptist, to receive Christian baptism? This incident is recorded in Acts 19:1-5a. "And it happened while Apollos was at Corinth, That Paul, having passed through the upper regions, came to Ephesus. And finding some disciples, he said to them, 'Did you receive the Holy Spirit when you believed?' So they said to him, 'We have not so much as heard whether there is a Holy Spirit.' And he said to them, 'Into what then were you baptized?' So they said, 'Into John's baptism.' Then Paul said, 'John indeed baptized with a baptism of repentance, saying to the people that they should believe on Him who would come after him, that is, on Christ Jesus.' When they heard this, they were baptized in the name of the Lord Jesus.

The Baptism of Jesus by John has another explanation and meaning which seems to satisfy Scripture more closely than saying it was an example for us to follow. When John baptized Jesus, he was doing this as both a prophet and a priest (which he was by inheritance from his father). The Scripture notes that Jesus was about thirty years old at the time. Think back with me to the time of King David. He was anointed to be King over Israel by Samuel, who was both prophet and priest. When David was thirty years of age, he was crowned as king over Judah alone, but it was seven years later before he entered into the office as King over all Israel. Jesus began

85

His kingdom with a small number of followers, but it was only after His ascension that He occupied the throne at God's right hand. It will be after His return in power and glory that to Him every knee will bow and every tongue confess that he is Lord. The similarities between David and Jesus are remarkable. Finally Mary was told that He would inherit the throne of David and would reign over the house of Jacob forever. I believe this is the better explanation of Jesus' baptism. The very word, Christ, means the Anointed One. Even as David was opposed by most of Israel, so our Lord Jesus met unending and growing hostility all the years of His earthly ministry.

Jesus was just beginning to enter His Messianic ministry. He went to Jerusalem to take part in His first Passover, after He began to gather His disciples and to proclaim His kingdom. When He entered the temple He found there a large and active commercial enterprise being conducted in the court of the Gentiles. The holy temple, dedicated to the worship of God, was filled with booths selling oxen, sheep and doves to the pilgrims who had come to offer their sacrifices to the Lord. He also found other booths used as money changers, for the pilgrims would have come from many nations in the empire. This was being justified as a convenience for the worshipers, but also as profitable for the high priests and scribes. This entire enterprise brought unbounded income to Annas, Caiaphas and their minions. Jesus had made deadly enemies. He made a scourge of small ropes plaited together and began to drive out the live stock and the merchants saying, "Take these things out! Make not My Father's house a place of merchandise!" The disciples who had come with Him remembered the Scripture that said, "Zeal for Thy house has consumed Me."

The angry priests and merchants confronted Him with these words; "What miraculous signs will You show us to justify Your actions?

Jesus answered back, "Destroy this temple and in three days I will raise it up." "Will you indeed?" they replied. "Forty-six years this temple was in process of being built, and you will raise it up in three days?" But he was speaking of the temple of His body. When He was raised from the dead, His disciples would remember that He had said this, and would then understand and believe.

Not all the pious Jews were happy about the desecration of the temple, and some would secretly applaud what Jesus had done. Among these was Nicodemus, a prominent teacher and highly regarded member of the ruling body, the Sanhedrin. He saw some of the signs that Jesus had performed, and had heard of many more. He was deeply impressed and wanted to know more. So he came to Jesus somewhat secretly, to question Him and to discover what new revelation He might bring from God. Nicodemus was not expecting the answer Jesus gave him.

Jesus went right to the heart of the matter by saying to him, "Except a man be born again, he cannot see the kingdom of God." Nicodemus knew Jesus was not talking about a second physical birth, but he thought that a new spiritual birth was just as impossible. So he asked, "How can a man be born when he is old?" Can he enter a second time into his mother's womb and be born?" Jesus patiently took him back to the Old Testament books of Jeremiah and Ezekiel (in which Nicodemus was supposed to be an expert), and reminded him of the promise God gave about a new heart which He would give to His people. He further explained how this would come about in these words; "For as Moses lifted up the serpent in the wilderness, even so must the Son of Man be lifted up, that whoever believes upon Him should not perish but should have eternal life."

This was the first direct reference Jesus made to the certainty and necessity of His own crucifixion. Nicodemus left the presence of Jesus probably still mystified, but, I think, deeply impressed with what he heard. Three years later, as he helped his friend, Joseph of Arimathea, bury the dead body of Jesus, which they had taken down from the cross, the words of Jesus on that night long ago would come to his mind. Now He would understand. Now he would believe. Now he would experience that new birth he thought was impossible. This new birth is still available to all who, with Nicodemus of old, will look to the lifted up Savior.

Shortly after this encounter with Nicodemus, Jesus, filled with the Holy Spirit and His power, began teaching in all the synagogues. His marvelous deeds and words preceded Him and He was received with enthusiasm, and was praised by all who heard Him—except in one place. He came to Nazareth where He was brought up; and as was His custom, He went into the synagogue and stood up to read the Holy Scripture. He read from the Isaiah scroll these words: "The Spirit of the Lord is upon me; because of this, He has anointed me. To publish glad news to the lowly has He sent me; to restore those broken in heart; to proclaim deliverance to the captives, and recovery of sight to the blind; to give liberty to the oppressed; to proclaim the acceptable year of the Lord…" Having read this text, He sat down, and said to those assembled there; "Today this Scripture has been fulfilled in your ears."

The response was rejection and angry irritation at His words. "Who does he think he is? We know Him. He is the son of Joseph, the carpenter, and now He is the carpenter, and he is claiming these things for Himself?" Jesus' response implied that He was a prophet of God, and like Elijah and Elisha of old, He was being rejected. And like these former prophets, He would turn to others beyond Israel, who would accept Him. This was too much! They rushed Him out of the synagogue and out of the city, intending to kill Him by hurling Him headlong off the cliffs overlooking Nazareth. However this was neither the time, nor place, nor manner of His death He must die. So He passed through their midst and left them to their murderous anger.

He continued His tour of Galilee, preaching the good news, healing the sick, casting out demons, and gathering disciples. He healed a man almost consumed by leprosy and His fame spread far and wide. Great multitudes followed Him, to hear Him preach and to be healed of their infirmities. Jesus was pressed hard to find time to be alone with the Father in prayer. Among the towns he visited was Capernaum. By this time, spies from the ruling class began to follow Him, trying their best to discredit Him, and even seeking evidence they might take back to the Sanhedrin in Jerusalem and bring formal charges against Him. His widespread popularity alarmed the high priests, and none of them would forget how He had disrupted the very profitable commerce in the temple. For this they would never forgive Him. They would seek cause for His death and continued in this quest for the next three years.

At one point some men brought to Jesus a paralyzed friend. To get near Jesus, they tore up the tiles of the roof over the place where He was teaching, and lowered the poor man down in front of Jesus, hoping for a miracle of healing. They found even more. When Jesus saw their faith He said to the paralytic, "Take courage young man, your sins are forgiven you." The spies began to whisper to each other, "We have Him now! He is speaking blasphemy. Who can forgive sins but God alone?"

Jesus, knowing their thoughts and hearing their whispers, confronted them with a certain amount of ironic humor. "Which is easier, to say to this paralytic, 'Your sins are forgiven you,' or to say, 'arise and take up your pallet and walk?'"Then sternly He said, "So that you may know that the Son of Man has authority on earth to forgive sins" (He said to the paralytic) "I say to you arise, take up your pallet and go home." Much to the amazement of all, he took up his pallet, and praising God aloud and unceasing, he returned to his home, whole and well in every way.

The spies fled to Jerusalem to report what they had heard and seen. The temple crowd was scandalized by what they heard, but Caiaphas was inwardly pleased. Jesus had begun to supply him with the evidence he would need for a trial and conviction on the charge of blasphemy—a capital offense.

About this same time, Jesus made another unforgivable "mistake," He enlisted a hated tax collector into His inner circle of disciples. That, too, would be used against Him, to turn the fickle, gullible public away from Him. The tide of rejection and deadly anger was rising, and would, in the end, overwhelm Him. The temple spies would follow Him everywhere, seeking more "evidence" to condemn Him.

On another Sabbath day, when He was teaching in a local synagogue, there was a man present who had a withered hand. The spies were present too, of course. It was probably they who had deliberately brought this man into the synagogue to test Jesus; they were so hard hearted. But unlike His accusers, Jesus' heart was filled with compassion. So these spies asked Him, "Is it lawful to heal on the Sabbath?" Jesus knew their thoughts and said to the man with the withered hand, "Rise up and stand before them." Jesus, addressing the spies, said to them, I will also ask you a question. Is it lawful on the Sabbath to do good- or to do evil? To save life- or to destroy it?" They refused to answer Him. So He asked again, "What man shall there be among you who shall have one sheep, and if it falls into a pit on the Sabbath, will not rescue it?" Then how much more is a man worth than a sheep! Therefore it is lawful to do good on the Sabbath." He looked upon these self-righteous men with anger and grief at their hardness of heart. He said to the man with the withered hand, "Stretch out your hand." And he obeyed Jesus and instantly his hand was restored.

When they heard what Jesus said, and saw this amazing miracle, they did not admit their own perfidy, nor did they rejoice over the healing. Rather they were filled with madness and began to consult with each other how they might use this deed to accuse Jesus of being a Sabbath breaker. Some of the Pharisees who were present held council and made common cause with the Herodians, so that together they might destroy Jesus. They saw no reason to rejoice over the incredible miracles of Jesus. They completely ignored His words of compassion and power. Their only thought was the danger He posed to their positions of power. Their only response was to plot and connive to put Him to death before the whole nation rose up and accepted His claim to be the Son of God, and the heir to David's throne. This they must prevent, or to be swept away into oblivion.

One of the most amazing of all the Messianic signs Jesus performed was the casting out of demons from a number of possessed people. None could deny that He had gloriously triumphed over evil spirit, and those folk who had been held in their power were delivered. This included a good number of prominent and well known women who had been set free. But the temple spies, and the scribes who been sent to follow Him around, had an answer for this. They widely proclaimed that Jesus could only cast out these evil spirits because he was in league with Beelzebul the Prince of all demons.

They spread abroad the ridiculous accusation saying, "He casts out the demons through the Prince of demons." Most people could see through this convoluted reasoning, but some believed it. So Jesus called these men before Him and spoke to them by analogies: "How can Satan cast out Satan" If a kingdom is divided against itself, that kingdom cannot stand. So if Satan has risen against himself, he cannot stand, but comes to an end." Then He warned them, who had accused Him of blasphemy, that they were dangerously close to committing the ultimate blasphemy by ascribing evil to the Holy Spirit. Which sin, said He, will never be forgiven in this world or in all eternity.

With the increasingly dangerous hostility of the leaders of the people, and with the widespread popularity of Jesus, His mother and His brothers and sisters were alarmed and fearful. They were even afraid that He had lost His mind. They wanted to talk with Him and take Him back home to protect and care for Him. There was such a large crowd around Him, His own family could not get close enough to speak with Him. Jesus was not callous towards His own kin, but neither could He give in to their desire. It is understandable that Mary, His mother, feared for Him, but had she forgotten all the words spoken to her by the Angel Gabriel, when he revealed to her who her Spirit-conceived son would be?

When Jesus returned to Judea and came to Jerusalem to keep one of the feasts of the Jewish people, He found a man waiting by a pool which reputedly had miraculous healing powers. But no one would help the man to enter the pool. This man had been crippled thirty-eight years! Jesus asked him, "Do you want to get well?" He answered, "There is no one to help me enter the pool in time to receive its healing powers." Jesus simply said to him, "Rise; take up your pallet and walk." The healing was complete and instant. No one was more surprised than he, when he found himself walking after all these long years. Almost immediately he was confronted by some of the scribes and Pharisees. "Don't you know it is unlawful for you to carry that pallet on the Sabbath?" The healed man told them, "The one who made me well, he said to me, 'take up your pallet and walk." "Who is this man?" they asked, but he did not know who Jesus was. A little later Jesus found him in the temple and said, "You have been healed; sin no more, lest, a worse thing happen to you." There is certainly at least a suggestion in the words of Jesus that the man's crippled condition was due to his sinful life style. When he heard this warning from Jesus, he went directly to the Jews and told them it was Jesus of Nazareth who made him well.

Once more, in their minds, Jesus had broken the Sabbath. Their anger increased along with their determination to kill Him. When they confronted Jesus with their accusation, His response infuriated them even more. "My Father is working until now, and I, too, am working." Now they were really incensed. By His words, Jesus was making it clear that He was truly the Son of God and had come from the Father to do His will. What they willingly overlooked was the evidence that Jesus' claims were validated by His deeds. The proper response would have been to accept the evidence and the claim and acknowledge the evident truth about Jesus. He went on to say that because he truly was the Son of God, the Father had given Him power and authority even to raise the dead. Then to these angry, self- righteous men, He issued this gracious offer: "Truly, truly I say to you, He who hears my word and believes Him who sent me, has everlasting life and does not come into judgment but has passed from death in to life." He went on to say, even more emphatically and urgently, "Truly I say to you that an hour is coming, and now is when the dead will hear the voice of the Son of God, and those who hear shall live...Marvel not at this, for an hour is coming when all who are in the graves will hear His voice and come forth; they that have done good into the resurrection of life, and they who have done evil unto resurrection of judgment. Jesus continued to press His claims and Himself on these stubborn men. He challenged them to go back to their Scriptures (the Old Testament) and to search them diligently that they might understand that He was the fulfillment of all things revealed about God in those Scriptures. With sadness and sober warning He added, "But you are unwilling to come to me that you might have life. Do not think that I will accuse you to the Father; no, it is Moses, in whom you claim to believe; he will accuse you; For if you had truly believed Moses, you would have believed me."

The encounter was over, for now, and they went their way to report to the high priest all that Jesus had said, and more determined than ever, that He must die for His impudent, arrogant claim to be the Son of God.

After this Jesus returned to Galilee, and once more went to the synagogue in His home town to teach and preach, with the same results as before. They simply would not believe, in spite of the abundant evidence, that He was anything more than a home town boy, and they rejected Him once more.

The story was different in the rest of Galilee. The people received Him gladly and observed with increasing wonder, the glory of His many miracles of healing. Jesus summoned His twelve special disciples, gave them great power to heal the sick, and to expel evil spirits, and commissioned them to preach the good news that the Kingdom of Heaven is at hand. It was about this time that King Herod had arrested and imprisoned John the Baptist for confronting him about his adulterous affair and marriage to Herodias, his brother's wife. Herod feared to kill John, but his paramour had no such hesitation. She connived to have Herod execute John, which he reluctantly did. Later, Herod would also play a minor role in the condemnation of Jesus.

When Jesus sent His disciples out on their first preaching tour, He warned them they would sheep among the wolves, in constant danger. Yet at the same time He encouraged them to be brave, and to rest in the assurance they were going out in His name and with the protection of the Father. He said, "If they hate you, they hated me first." "Do not fear", said He, "and do not fear those who kill the body but are unable to kill the soul." With many other words of instruction and warnings, He sent them out endowed with great spiritual power, and their mission was met with great success as they proclaimed the glad news everywhere.

When the disciples returned, they all gathered together and reported with joy on what God had done through them. Jesus joined them in their rejoicing, and said to them, "Come away by yourselves to a quiet place and rest a while." He took them in a small boat to the other side of the Sea of Galilee to escape the press of the crowd. But it was not to be. The crowds learned where they were going, and from all over Galilee the people traveled to that secluded spot bringing with them all the sick, the lame and the demon possessed. Rather than being irritated, the Lord welcomed them, taught them the truths of the kingdom and healed all their sick. The day was almost over, and still the vast multitude crowded around Jesus, with moiré and more people coming.

Jesus began to test His disciples by asking, "Where shall we buy bread to feed such a multitude?" The disciples were troubled and perplexed asking, "How could we feed such a crowd? Even if we had two hundred denaries, that would not buy enough for such a crowd." But Andrew had found a small boy with a small lunch which he had offered, "but" said Andrew, "what are these among so many?" Jesus took the small bag of food, commanded the disciples to have the men sit in companies of fifty and hundreds, He and began to break the loaves and the two small fish and give it to the thousands gathered there by the lake. When He had finished, they found that all had been fed, and an abundance left over.

The people saw the connection between what Moses had done many centuries before; how he had fed the multitudes on the Manna God sent from heaven. They were ready to make Jesus their King, by force, if need be. So He sent the disciples back across the lake in their boat, while He went away into the mountains to pray alone. During the storm tossed night which followed, the disciple found themselves on a very rough sea, in a very small boat. Jesus went to their rescue, but that is another story to be considered at another time, perhaps.

The next morning the crowds found Jesus again and were determined to make Him their King. When Jesus explained to them the nature of His kingdom, and when He offered Himself to them as the "bread of life", they quickly lost interest in Him and His kingdom. From this point on, it was not just the jealous leaders who rejected Jesus, but also many of the great multitudes who had so enthusiastically sought Him out at first after seeing His many miracles. Before another day had ended, those who had demanded Him to be their King, now deserted Him in droves. The tide of rejection and deep anger now came rushing in on Jesus. This would soon culminate in His trial, conviction and death. Every healing He effected, every leper He cleansed, every hungry one He fed, every demon He cast out; all of these gracious and powerful acts of Jesus brought Him one step nearer the day of His death. In the fullest sense of the word, He bore our sins and our infirmities. He knew this, of course, "For the Son of Man came to seek and to save that which was lost." In the very end, it was only His heart-breaking separation from the Father, that would enable the Apostle Paul to later write, "For I am convinced that neither death, nor life, nor angels, nor principalities, nor things present, nor things to come, nor powers, nor height, nor depth, nor any other created thing, shall be able to separate us from the love of God, which is in Christ Jesus our Lord."

Even though He had been rejected at Capernaum, He remained in Galilee, being unwilling to return to Judea, because there was a determination among the leadership in Jerusalem to put Him to death. This would happen of course, but "His time was not yet", so he continued His ministry in Galilee. Even in Galilee, the Pharisees continued to follow Him around, building their case for getting rid of Him. They assailed Him for not following "in the traditions of the elders," and not requiring His disciples to do so.

At one point, after hearing their bitter accusations against Him, Jesus responded to them by saying, "You hypocrites! Well did Isaiah prophesy concerning you, when he said, as it is written, 'With their mouths do this people draw near to me, and with their lips, they honor Me, but their heart is far off from Me; in vain are they worshiping Me, teaching as doctrines, the *commandments of men*." Then Jesus called out to all who had gathered around to hear this confrontation, "Hear me, all of you, and understand: there is nothing from without a man, going into his mouth can defile him; but the things coming out of his mouth, it is they that defile him." The disciples seemed unsure of what He meant until He explained further in simple, straightforward language. "The things which go forth from the mouth of a man come from the heart, and these defile a man." Later, they would remember these words and write them down for our benefit.

While still in Galilee, Jesus began to reach out to the Gentiles living in that section of the country. He healed their sick and demon possessed, He fed their hungry too, as He had fed the Galileans. None of this was lost on His enemies. They saw it all, and reported back to their leaders. The case for His execution was becoming stronger and stronger; at least in their evil minds.

One of the major celebrations of the Jewish people was drawing near. Jesus' blood brothers taunted Him saying, "Leave here and go to Judea that your disciples may see the many works you are doing. No one who wants to be known publicly does his works in secret. Go ahead and display yourself where it will really count, in Jerusalem." They were embarrassed by Jesus' words and deeds and wanted Him to leave their area. They did not accept His claims, nor believe in Him. Jesus responded to their taunts, "You go, My time is not yet here. But your time is always ready. The world does not hate you; but it does hate Me, because I testify of it, that its works are evil. The day would soon come when His brothers would see and understand just how deadly the world's hatred of their elder brother would be.

Down in Jerusalem, there was divided opinion concerning Jesus. Some were saying, "He is a good a man", but others were saying, "No, He is deceiving the people." They all knew the leaders were plotting His death, and wonder why they were delaying His arrest. In fact, at that very festive celebration, the Sanhedrin sent officers to arrest Jesus; but when they heard so many people saying of Him that He was either a great prophet, or maybe even the Messiah, they dared not arrest Him publicly.

Once more he offered Himself openly to the Jewish leadership saying, "I am telling you only what the Father has told me to say, and yet you are seeking to kill Me, because you are obeying your Father." Abraham is our father" they claimed. "If Abraham was truly your Father, you would do his works, and believe in Me. If God was your father, you would have believed in Me and loved Me, for I came from God, and He it was who sent me to you. I did not come on My own, but He, the Father sent Me. You, on the other hand, are of your father, the Devil, and his works you do." "You have a demon", they screamed at Jesus. "No, I do not have a demon, I am honoring My Father and offering you eternal life. If anyone believes and keeps My word, he shall never die." They had Him now! This was the last straw. "Now we know you have a demon! Abraham died, and the prophets died, yet you claim, 'If anyone keeps My words, he shall not taste death forever.' Are you greater than Abraham and the prophets? Just who do you think you are?" "If I told you that I did not know the Father, I would be a liar…like you. But I do know Him and keep His word. Your father, Abraham rejoiced in that he would see My day; and he saw it, and was glad."

The Jews laughed Him to scorn. "You are not yet fifty years old; and you have seen Abraham?" Jesus replied earnestly, "Truly, truly I say to you, 'before Abraham was, I AM.'" In uncontrollable rage, they sought for stones to stone Him to death. But while they were finding their stones, Jesus slipped quietly away. Once more, this was neither the time, the place, nor the manner in which Jesus was destined to die.

Their case against Jesus was building. They would not forget what He said about Himself, nor would they forget that He had said to them, "You are of your father the devil, and his works you do." That was unforgivable. "He escaped this time, but not forever, and not for long."

The struggle continued as Jesus opened the eyes of a man who had been born blind. No one had ever seen or heard of a man born blind being healed. Jesus did this after saying that this was the kind of work the Father had sent Him into the world to do. He also made mentioned that the "day time" of His work was drawing to an end, and that night (His death) would soon come. In the minds of the Pharisees, Jesus had committed the unforgivable sin. He had healed the blind man on the Sabbath. Many people had witnessed this great sign, even Jesus' most bitter enemies. However, no one, not even the healed blind man, could deny that it was on the Sabbath; and no one could deny that this blind-from-birth man was now seeing.

The Pharisees questioned the man over and over trying to find a way to condemn him. They even questioned his parents, unconvinced that he had actually been blind. These folks, frightened as they were over being questioned by the officials, affirmed that this man was their son, and that he had been born blind. However, they would not affirm that Jesus was the one who opened his eyes, for they knew they would be expelled from the synagogue if they gave credit to Jesus. Their son, the one who had been born blind, weary of their unending questions, not only told them again that Jesus had healed him, but that He obviously had been sent from God. "This is truly a marvel", he said, "that do not know that he had come from God, for no one has ever opened the eyes of a man born blind, have they? He must have come from God!" In great anger they officially expelled him from the synagogue. When Jesus heard of it, He went to the man and led him to believe that He was truly the Son of God, the Messiah. The healed man bowed in worship and confessed Him saying, "Lord I believe." For this blessed and fortunate man, a new day in his life had begun. For Jesus, this kind deed brought Him one step nearer death.

Yet as the Good Shepherd of His Sheep, He was ready to lay down His life for those the Father had given Him, and He knew that day would soon come. He said an amazing thing in the presence of those seeking to kill Him. "No one is taking My life away from Me. I am laying it down of my will. I have the authority to lay it down, and authority to claim it again. This authority has been given Me from My Father." They demanded, "If you are the Messiah, tell us plainly." Jesus answered truthfully, "I have told you and shown you that I am He, and you do not believe Me." He went on to say, "MY sheep hear My voice, and I know them, and they follow Me. I give them eternal life and they shall never perish, nor shall anyone snatch them out of My hand. My Father who gave them to Me is greater than all, and no one can snatch them for the hand of the Father." What assurance this must have brought to the blind man He had healed, and who had been expelled from the synagogue. Then He added, "I and the Father are one.

The time was rapidly drawing near when He would be condemned and crucified. More and more Jesus was teaching His disciples what lay ahead for Him, and for them. They did not fully understand what he was telling them, and of course they did not want these things to happen to their Lord, or to them. When He asked them what people were saying about Him, they answered that they thought He was one of the great prophets from of old who had come back again. They did not mention what His enemies were saying about Him. Jesus pressed the point even further and asked what they thought of Him. Simon Peter immediately responded, "You are the Christ, the Son of God." We have looked at that scene in an earlier chapter, but the point here is that Jesus responded quickly to that confession of Peter by telling him this was a truth that came from God. Peter, no doubt, was beaming with pride when he heard Jesus commend him. What Peter did not expect or want to hear was what followed. "Because I am the Messiah" said Jesus, in effect, "I must go to Jerusalem, suffer many things, and be rejected by the elders, scribe s and chief priests, and I will be killed, but rise from the dead on the third day."

They were all stunned and horrified. This was no veiled allusion; this was outright, forthright and plain. It was more than Peter could accept. He protested vigorously, saying none of these things could possibly happen to Jesus. But Jesus warned Peter that he was thinking as the world thinks, and was not thinking God's thoughts. Then as if to convince Peter and the others that these things must be to fulfill all Scripture, He took Peter, James and John into a high mountain to pray. While Jesus was praying, He was transformed before them. His face began to shine as the sun, and even His clothing became brilliant and filled with light. Suddenly there appeared two men from the past, Moses and Elijah. They too, were shiningly bright. They were talking with Jesus about what would happen to Him in Jerusalem. I think this was the Lord's way of confirming that His coming death had been in the plan of God, and revealed, at least in part, in the Old Testament Scriptures. Peter, in his stammering way, wanted to keep Jesus, Moses and Elijah before them for all time. In the midst of this wonder, a voice came from the bright cloud saying, "This is My beloved Son in whom I delight, hearken unto Him." When the earthly life and ministry of Jesus would come to an end, these three men and all the rest of the disciples would remember and would understand the perfect plan of God as revealed not only in the death of Jesus, but even more in His glorious resurrection.

Not long after this, Jesus brought up the subject of His approaching death again. He said to His faithful followers, "Let these words sink into your ears: for the Son of Man is going to be delivered into the hands of (evil) men, and they will kill Him: and after He is killed, He will be raised up on the third day." They were deeply distressed. They still did not understand what he was dying, or how this could possibly happen to Him.

For the last time, Jesus left Galilee, and began to move determinedly towards Jerusalem. On this last journey, which would last for several weeks, He performed many miracles and continued to teach and instruct His disciples in the things of the kingdom. During these times of teaching, He would again resort to simple stories as illustrations of eternal truths. His disciples noted that He spent much time in prayer, so they asked again, as they had much earlier, "Lord, teach us to pray." He once more went back to what He had taught them in the words of what we now call, "The Lord's Prayer." He spent much time teaching them the importance of forgiveness in their dealing with one another.

The scribes and Pharisees who had been harassing Him during most of His ministry, said to Him, "We want to see some miraculous sign from You; some sign from heaven itself." They implied, that if He would only show them some great sign, they would believe. They lied! Soon He would show them great signs including raising up Lazarus who had been dead four days, but they did not believe. He would show them the ultimate sign from heaven; His own resurrection. Still, they did not believe

The story of Lazarus, and his return from the dead by the command of Jesus was known far and wide by many people. Instead of leading them to believe In Him, it only confirmed in the leaders the growing determination n to kill Jesus, and to do it very soon. As Caiaphas points out to them, "It's Him or us, all of us, How much better for one man to perish than for the whole nation to be destroyed." So they acknowledged this great miracle that it had happened, but they missed the meaning of it and continued on their willful way. Before much longer, the Romans did indeed invade in force and destroyed the nation. The walls of Jerusalem were torn down and the temple lay in ruins, never again to be rebuilt.

The time for the final Passover before the death of Jesus was at hand. Jesus made one final appearance and appeal to the people of the Holy City. He gave them a sign from heaven. He rode into the city on a small donkey, the symbol of peace. Even as the Prophet Zechariah had foretold. "Behold your King is coming to you… humble and mounted on a donkey, even on a colt, the foal of a donkey." The rulers of Judea ignored the sign, missed its meaning, and ignored their King. For a brief moment the crowds of common people who had come for the Passover caught on and hailed Jesus as he entered the city. That, too, soon passed, and the last few days of conflict between Jesus and the blind leaders of the blind intensified, until the betrayer made his nefarious bargain with the wicked men of the Sanhedrin, and Jesus was sentenced to die by way of crucifixion. The tide of rejection and bitter hatred had at last submerged the Son of Man. The dreadful darkness which overtook Him on the cross seemed to confirm that he had been defeated. The Father had hidden His face from Him and there was darkness over all the land.

But this was not the end of His story.

7

Mystery of Judas Iscariot

Judas Iscariot, who was one of the special twelve Jesus chose to be His disciples, is remembered down through human history for one thing and one thing only... he betrayed Jesus of Nazareth for a hand full of silver coins. This crime erases all the good things he might have ever done. He is not remembered for being chosen by Christ. He is not remembered for preaching the good news of the kingdom. He is not remembered for casting out demons or healing all manner of diseases, which he did. He is not remembered for being the only Judean chosen by Christ. He is not even remembered for being one of the twelve who chose to remain with Jesus when thousands turned away and walked with Him no more. The list of "good things" could go on and on, but why bother? Take all of these things and whatever else your imagination might serve up and blot them out; his one foul deed outweighs all else. He betrayed Jesus to death and stands condemned, even by the unbelieving world, for this inexcusable act.

There are special cells in places of incarceration in which prisoners may be placed for their own protection from the wrath and anger of other prisoners for deeds so heinous and despicable that even hardened criminals will not accept. Will Judas Iscariot have to endure being cast into outer darkness alone in his remorse and torment? How many will share a like fate? We are not given to know the inner workings of Judas' mind and heart; we may only observe and hopefully learn from his actions. It is painful to look at Judas and think of his atrocious deed of betrayal. It is painful also to look at ourselves and see some of the sins in our own lives which we share with Judas. Was he a self centered person? So am I. Was he driven by desire to be on what he thought would be the "winning side"? Was he disillusioned when he saw the inevitable "defeat" of Jesus? Was he fearful lest he too might be caught up in the same net and meet the same fate?

The Bible is, among other things, a mirror in which we may see ourselves. We see some of the same sins in ourselves that we see so plainly in Judas and know unless grace truly grips us and frees us we could also share in the sins and fate of Judas. As Chaplain Michael Cannon so aptly said in his book, The Trials and Passion of Christ; "…Every man has his Judas in his own life. Every man will experience one whom he brings into his confidence, brings into his trust, who will prove untrustworthy and who will be a traitor. Every person has his or her Judas; every church has its Judas…and I am almost as convinced that every man has the potential to be a Judas; every one of us has the potential to be a betrayer."

Many articles and many books have been written in an attempt to explain the mind and reasoning of Judas Iscariot. His actions and his personality and inner motivation have been examined and explained over and over again by those who never knew the man, but think that some deep, inner and unknown motivations were driving him. A few of these biographies have attempted to explain his behavior and even excuse him from the blame and infamy which we associate with his name. Some years ago I read a book with the intriguing title, A Tear for Judas, in which the author attempted to explain that Judas was really motivated by a desire to force Jesus to show His hand and assert His authority. The book was well written, but the effort fell short of being convincing. There have been other books and commentaries which have tried to at least partially excuse Judas on the grounds his motivation was really somewhat noble and idealistic though misguided. All of these efforts are based on mere speculation or the modern tendency to blame bad behavior on unfortunate circumstances earlier in life.

From the earliest days of Christianity there have even been those who were so appalled by Judas' betrayal of Jesus that they thought that no human being could commit such a criminal act; so Judas must have been a demon sent from hell in the form of a man. This view fails to take into account the biblical teaching on the depravity of fallen human nature and the depth of evil to which that depravity may lead one. From a human perspective there have been many, many actors on the stage of the human drama whose cruelty and inhumanity seem far worse than Judas' infamous deed, as horrible as it was. But in a sense Judas stands alone as the personification of treachery and base betrayal. So far the question, "Why did Judas betray Jesus of Nazareth unto death?" remains unanswered. There is a trail of evidence which points to the answer, which is not nearly so complicated as many would have us believe. Let us follow that trail and see the reasons plainly given for Judas' betrayal of Christ.

Part of the mystery of Judas was why he was chosen by Christ to be one of the inner circle of His followers. The answer to that question remains a mystery. Jesus Himself never explained his choice, but it is evident that Jesus knew long before Judas knew, that he would betray Jesus and would be destroyed by his base conduct. Early in His ministry Jesus had fed five thousand people with just a handful of food. When the people wanted to take Jesus and force him to become their king, Jesus withdrew and crossed the lake to the other side. The multitudes followed Him, apparently still intent on making Him their king. Jesus used the occasion to explain the nature of His kingdom and the deeper meaning of being His disciples. He told them, in effect, that they must understand that he Himself was the true bread of life and that they must feast on Him to be part of His kingdom. He said, "I am the Bread of Life. He who comes to me shall never hunger and he who believes on me shall never thirst...for my flesh is food indeed and my blood drink indeed. He who eats my flesh and drinks my blood dwells in me and I in him...he who eats this bread shall live forever." At this saying many of His would-be disciples went away and followed Him no more. And he was left with primarily the 12 inner circle of disciples. He said to the departing crowds, "But there are some of you who believe not."

For Jesus knew from the very first who they were who did not believe, and who it was that would betray Him." Jesus chose Judas to be one of the favored few and he gave every indication of being a true disciple; but Jesus knew his heart.

We note from this point on the gradual decline of Judas into complete apostasy, and the steps which led in that direction. Dr William Hendriksen said of Judas and his fall: "What caused this privileged disciple to become Christ's betrayer? Was it injured pride, disappointed ambition, deeply entrenched greed, fear of being put out of the synagogue? No doubt all of these were involved, but could not the most basic reason have been this, that between the utterly selfish heart of Judas and the infinitely unselfish and outgoing heart of Jesus there was a chasm so immense that either Judas must implore the Lord to bestow upon him the grace of regeneration and renewal, a request the betrayer refused to make, or else he must offer his help to get rid of Jesus." In the end, the latter was his choice.

As the inevitable end drew near, apparently the bitterness of Judas began to control him utterly. Like the other disciples he had eagerly responded to the call of Christ, and was excited about the prospect of the glorious Messianic kingdom. No doubt he (and they) were confused at times and disappointed that Jesus did not begin the uprising that would rid the nation of the hated Romans and usher in the long awaited kingdom. Judas and all the rest of them looked forward to places of honor and power within that kingdom. James and John, through their mother, requested the right to sit on His right and left hands when he ascended the throne. Judas was sure the office of treasurer awaited him. From the earliest days of Jesus' ministry, Judas had been in charge of the meager funds available to Jesus and His disciples. As the time went on, the initial enthusiasm began to wear thin. Even though Jesus continued to work miraculous signs, opposition to Him and His ministry was growing among the elite and the powerful in Judah especially in Jerusalem. The confidence of Judas and many others in Jesus and His kingdom began to wane. This was at least partially the result of Jesus' increasingly frequent warnings about what awaited Him in the holy city. He used such terms as rejected, suffering, death by crucifixion, and other somber words. Most of the disciples seemed to think that Jesus was speaking metaphorically, but probably Judas began to think Jesus meant these things would actually happen to Him. He even used the term "betrayal" over and over again.

Then an incredible thing happened that was absolutely astounding! Jesus raised Lazarus from the dead even after his body had been in the tomb four days! Since this occurred just a short distance from Jerusalem, the news spread rapidly and was all the talk of the people near and far. There was great consternation among the Jewish rulers. Later John would write in his Gospel: "So the chief Priests and the Pharisees gathered the Council (the Sanhedrin) and said, 'What are we to do? For this man (Jesus) is performing many miraculous signs. If we let Him go on like this, all men will believe in Him and the Romans will come and take away both our place and even our nation.' But a certain one of them, Caiaphas, who was High Priest that year, said to them ' you know nothing at all, nor do you take into account that it is expedient for you that one man should die for the people, and that the whole nation should not perish.'" From that day on, they planned to kill Jesus of Nazareth and began to make definite plans how this could be done without arousing the whole population, lest there be a riot which would end with the Sanhedrin being dissolved by the Roman authorities. The chief priests and the Pharisees gave orders that if anyone knew where Jesus was he should report it at once so they might arrest Him with as little public knowledge as possible. No doubt the word was spread and Judas would have known about this. Thoughts were beginning to form in his mind which soon would become a plan of action.

The opportunity came when Jesus and His disciples were invited to the home of Mary, Martha, and Lazarus for a dinner of celebration over the return of Lazarus from the grave. At this feast of gratitude Mary, the sister of Lazarus, brought out a box of very costly perfume and poured it on the feet of Jesus, wiping His feet with her hair. It was a beautiful expression of gratitude and devotion. For not only had Jesus raised her brother from the dead, but had raised her faith to a new height. But for Judas it was the last straw in a rage of growing fury. He had been frustrated and angry that all his plans for advancement and grandeur had been slipping away. As keeper of the meager resources available to Jesus and His disciples,

establishment had actually set up this business of selling the animals and exchanging the money right in the temple complex itself. Long before, one of the Hebrew prophets had written of the temple, "My house shall be called for all the nations a house of prayer." When Jesus entered Jerusalem to the wild acclaim of the multitudes, He went directly to the temple and began to drive out all those buying and selling. He over turned their money exchanging tables and brought the accusation by quoting the ancient prophet saying, "My house shall be called for all nations a house of prayer", and adding, "But you have made it a den of robbers." The crowds loved it, but it proved to the establishment to be an unforgivable sin which must be punished severely and soon lest they lose this lavish income. He must be eliminated and now!

This brave deed of Jesus gave Him the audience and the opportunity to proclaim His message of the Gospel to many people. The leaders did not immediately try to stop Him, for they greatly feared the people who at this point regarded Him as a great prophet, at least, and maybe even the long-awaited Messiah. But they continued to plot and frantically seek a way to eliminate him quietly. Judas saw all this and decided the time was ripe to go to these leaders secretly and offer them a plan to seize and arrest Jesus without arousing the wrath of the multitudes. He knew where Jesus was spending the night outside the city, and when he would go there. So he went to the authorities with his offer saying, "What will you give me if I deliver Him unto you?" I think it was Judas who suggested the amount, based on his anger at losing his rightful share of the three hundred denarii which had been wasted on the feet of Jesus. The leaders were jubilant and promised to give him what he asked, thirty pieces of silver. From that moment on, Judas had made himself a servant of evil and the Evil One, though he would never have admitted it. He left that secret rendezvous and began seeking opportunity to betray Him conveniently to them in the absence of the multitudes. At the same time Judas had to pretend that he was still a loyal follower of Jesus and went through all the expected motions of this. He was in on the plans for the Passover feast with Jesus and the rest of the twelve, confident that no one would even suspect him of any perfidy. He was right up to a point, with one exception…Jesus knew and had known all along, because he knew the heart of Judas.

The events began to unfold and rush towards the terrible climatic moment of betrayal. The poignant scene of the last supper began to unfold as Jesus sent His disciples to make proper preparation for the Passover meal. It was Thursday evening, Jesus' last day before his death. It is obvious that Judas attended this celebration of the Passover, at least the first part of it, but it is equally obvious that he left before the celebration ended and did not take part in the initial Lord's Supper which was to replace the ancient Passover celebration.

The disciples to whom Jesus had given the responsibility carried out His directions, and the sacred meal began. The Lord was filled with deep emotions. He was very much aware of what would happen this very night and how he would be betrayed and arrested. He told His disciples how much he had longed for this last Passover meal before His suffering would begin. His heart was overflowing with love for his faithful ones and heart sick over the one who would betray Him. In the Gospel of John we read these words: "So with the supper begun, though the Devil had already put it into the heart of Judas Iscariot, Simon's son to betray Him…Jesus rose from the supper and laid aside his garments and girded a towel about Himself. Then He poured water into a basin and began to wash the disciples' feet and to wipe them with the towel with which He was girded. He came therefore to Simon Peter; and

Peter said to Him, 'Lord, are you washing my feet?' Jesus answered him, 'What I am doing now you do not understand, but you will understand hereafter.' Peter said to Him, 'never will you wash my feet!' Jesus answered him, 'If I do not wash you, you have no part in Me.' Simon Peter said to Him, 'Lord, not my feet only but also my hands and my head.' Jesus said to him, 'He who has bathed needs not to wash-except his feet-but is clean all over. And you disciples are clean, though not all you.' (For he knew who was going to betray Him; it was for this He said, 'Not all of you are clean.'")

After Jesus had rejoined His disciples in the Passover meal, He stressed the importance of their understanding the meaning of what He had just done. "You call me Teacher and Lord...and so I am. If I then, your Teacher and Lord have washed your feet, you also ought to wash one another's feet." Though many Christians take this literally and practice foot washing as a ceremony, Jesus was probably thinking more about an attitude of loving, humble service of which He was and is the example, par excellence. He added, "If you know these things, blessed are you if you do them. I do not speak of all of you; I know those whom I chose. But it is that the Scripture may be fulfilled, 'He who eats bread with me lifted up his heel against me.'"

After Jesus said these things, He began to be deeply distressed and heartbroken. Then he said, "Verily, verily I say to you, that one of you will betray me-one who is eating with me." They all began to ask Him, "Lord is it I?" (looking at each other, deeply perplexed and grieved.) Judas somehow managed to appear equally perplexed and concerned. He even asked Jesus directly, "Rabbi, is it I?"Jesus simply replied; "It is as you have said." But only Judas and Jesus knew that it was indeed him. Perhaps Jesus' words about the betrayer being one who was dipping in the dish with Him confused them, for all of them had done this. Just then Jesus took a morsel of bread, dipped it in the dish of herbs and seasoning and gave it to Judas, saying, "What you are doing, do quickly." Again none of the others caught on and thought Jesus meant either go give something to the poor, as was sometimes done in the celebration of the Passover, or else that He meant, "go and buy some more food for the feast."

Judas left, and John appends, "and it was night." Indeed it was night, deep night in the mind and heart of Judas. I think he probably took the money bag with him to make sure none of the others would not discover the thirty pieces of silver. His next move is somewhat speculation but definitely implied. He went back to those who paid him to let them know where Jesus was. He also would have told them that if He had left the upper room, the site of the Passover meal, He would be going to the secluded garden called Gethsemane. In either case when the arresting officers found him, even if in the darkened garden, Judas would identify Him with a greeting and a kiss.

And so it was, Jesus had time to finish his instructions and admonitions to the disciples, spoken either in the upper room or as they journeyed to the garden. There Jesus began the ordeal of preparation in prayer for the unthinkable and dreaded. While He was giving himself over to the will and eternal plan of the Father to become truly "The Lamb of God who would take away the sin of the world," Judas was leading the temple guards and the Roman officers in their search for Jesus. If they had first gone to the location where Jesus and His disciples had celebrated the Passover, they now came to the garden just as Jesus had completed his prayer of complete surrender to the will of the Father and had accepted "the cup" He knew He must drink. There was confusion and consternation in that poignant scene. The disciples of Jesus were trying to stay awake. The traitor and the arresting band were just arriving with their torches and weapons, and in the midst of all there was Jesus who said to Judas, "Friend, for what purpose have you come?" Judas went directly up to Jesus and greeted Him warmly with a kiss and said, "Hail, Master!" Jesus responded, "Judas, are you betraying the Son of man with a kiss?" Then, as if to show Judas that his treachery was futile, He addressed the arresting officers saying, "Whom do you seek?" They answered, "Jesus of Nazareth." Jesus simply said, "I am he." Surprised, they drew away and fell to the ground. Was this only a reaction of surprise, or was this a way of showing who was really in charge? Jesus repeated His question and once more they said "Jesus of Nazareth." Jesus told them again that he was the one they were seeking and added, "Let these go away," pointing to His disciples. When His disciples would have defended him, even with arms, Jesus told them to put away their swords, and even healed the officer whom Simon Peter had wounded with his sword. Being unable to defend Him or themselves, the disciples all forsook Him and fled away into the darkness; and Jesus was led away to the trials which would condemn Him.

Judas no doubt tagged along and no doubt began to understand what he had done and the futility of his actions and behavior. Maybe he was trying to convince himself that he didn't really want Jesus to be condemned to death, only warned and sent back to Galilee. But I think he knew better and would face the harsh reality of what he had done when Jesus was condemned and sentenced to death by crucifixion. Maybe there was a voice within him frantically saying, "Go to Him, seek forgiveness and repent. Had not Jesus stressed the need for forgiveness? Had he not promised that all manner of sin, even against the Son of Man would be forgiven?" But he also remembered Jesus saying earlier this same evening, "Woe unto that man by whom the Son of Man is betrayed. It would be good for that man if he had never been born." The awful consequences had begun and he was undone. "What will I do if they condemn Him to death?" He would wait and see. He began to remember not only the powerful words of Jesus but also his many marvelous works of healing, His compassion towards the outcasts and the down trodden. He remembered all those intriguing parables he told, and the gentle way He dealt with those overtaken by habits and deeds of sin. He could almost see Jesus in his mind's eye picking up little children and cuddling them as He spoke tender words to them and to their parents. Would he ever forget hearing Him cry out, "Lazarus, come forth!"? And then the awesome spectacle of that man, who had been dead four days, walking out of the tomb in his grave wrappings. Surely some of those serving on the Sanhedrin would come to His defense. Surely they would not go before the Roman governor and seek the death penalty. Or would they? He also began to remember the anger, the rejection of Him and His doctrine, the hatred expressed over and over again by the leaders. He also was aware of the official warnings, posted everywhere that anyone who accepted Jesus as the Messiah would be cast out of the Synagogue or cast into prison. The mind of Judas was in a turmoil. What would he do? What could he do to make up for his betrayal?

Then the dreadful unthinkable happened. Jesus had been brutally beaten by the members of the Sanhedrin. They had condemned Him to death and were on their way to seek confirmation of their decision from Pilate and to demand His crucifixion. The burden of the thirty pieces of silver he had been paid weighed even more heavily upon his abused and self-wounded conscience. Suddenly it became clear to the tortured mind of Judas. He would return the money they had paid him. That would fix everything. Then he would quietly slip away and just return to his former life. Maybe he could join one of those outlaw bands that plotted the overthrow of the Romans and set Judah free. After all that was his hope when he followed Jesus of Nazareth.

Judas hurried to the temple and found some of the priests and elders of the Sanhedrin and tried to give back the money they had given him in the nefarious covenant of betrayal. Those men mocked Judas and refused to accept the thirty pieces of silver. When he said, "I have sinned by betraying innocent blood," they replied, "That's nothing to us, you take care of that." Judas in desperation threw down the money and fled the temple. Where could be go? What could he do? Then it dawned on him, "I can never undo what I have done. Somehow I must atone for my terrible sin." But there was nothing Judas could do to atone for his sin, and he had rejected the only way his guilty soul could be made free, when he turned his heart away from the "Lamb of God who takes away the sin of the world." In the madness of his mind and soul he made his way to the cliffs overlooking the valley, found a tree on the overhang, tied a cord around his neck, and leaped off to death. The cord held just long enough for his neck to break and his guilty soul to flee his body. Then the cord broke and his dead body fell hundreds of feet to be ghastly broken on the sharp rocks below. He left behind his name which would become a synonym for the most foul deed ever committed, and his soul met his maker.

The Trial and Tears of Peter

A big, brawny dangerous man had been driven too far. His fists were clinched, ready to strike. He was frustrated, angry and almost desperate. Nothing had worked out as he had hoped. He was being goaded and mocked by those who had joined him around the flickering fire in the courtyard just outside the palace of the High Priest where Jesus of Nazareth was being interrogated. His accusers had already decided He was guilty and deserving of death. No one was sure who this big man was, but many suspected that he was somehow connected with the Nazarene being questioned inside. Several of these bystanders were sure he was a friend and follower of Jesus and kept trying to get him to admit it. One man, whose kinsman had been severely wounded as the guards were arresting Jesus, was sure Peter was the one who had wounded him. But Peter denied all these accusations. His fear and anger became one explosive emotion, and he had had enough! The last accusation was made by a servant girl, maybe the one minding the gate when Peter was allowed to enter the courtyard. "This man was one of them" Once more Peter denied, saying, "I am not!" But they would not leave him alone. They all began to accuse him of being a follower of Jesus. At this point, angry beyond control, Simon Peter vehemently denied these accusations cursing and saying, "I don't even know this man of whom you speak. I don't know what you are talking about." The flickering flames of the warming fire in the courtyard were reflected in the angry, red face of Peter. He was ready to strike anyone who came near.

Then two things happened simultaneously; far off a crowing rooster was heard, and Jesus emerged from the door just in time to hear Peter's latest denial. As He turned and looked full in the face of Peter, that angry man suddenly remembered a warning Jesus had given him earlier in the evening. "Verily, verily, I say to you, Peter, the cock will not at all crow this day until you have denied three times that you know Me." Peter's response had been, "Lord I will follow you though all others forsake you. I will lay down my life for Your sake!" And he meant it, sincerely and fervently. But he had overestimated his own courage and strength and underestimated the wiles of Satan. He had forgotten that Jesus had warned him as they were eating the Passover meal that Satan greatly desired to see Peter fall. "Simon, Simon," said Jesus; "Satan demanded to have you that he might sift you as wheat, but I have prayed for you that your faith may not fail." The pained look in Jesus' already bruised and bloody face as He heard Peter's vehement denial brought back all these words to Peter's tortured mind. He burst into tears and fled away into the darkness. All of his self confidence had been swept away. The full realization of what he had done came crashing down on him. He had denied his Lord at just the time when Jesus would need him most. He, Simon the bold, Simon the brave, whom Jesus had named Peter, the rock, had openly denied Jesus! The other disciples, except for John, had forsaken Him and fled, but not Simon Peter. He had said to Jesus, "Though all others may forsake you, I will never forsake You. I am prepared to go to prison with you and to death if need be." How could it happen? "How could I have denied Him?"

As he sat alone in the darkness of night and in the greater darkness of failure, he began to remember many things. He remembered that day so long ago when the great prophet John the Baptist had pointed out Jesus and said of Him, "Behold the Lamb of God who takes away the sin of the world." He was not quite sure what John meant by those words, but he thought about them time and again as he went about his work as a commercial fisherman. He also began to hear marvelous things about this man, Jesus. He often saw Him walking close by the lake as Peter and his brother Andrew plied their trade of fishing with large nets. People said he had healed many sick folk and had even expelled demons! Could he possibly be the Messiah the prophets had promised? He had preached in several synagogues including the synagogue of Capernaum where Simon and his brother Andrew went each Sabbath to worship, study and pray. There again Jesus had spoken with great authority, and there He had again cast demons from a man. Simon had heard that man (or the demon within him) say, "I know who you are, the Holy One of God." He had felt a sense of awe and wonder. "Please come home with me," he heard himself saying to Jesus. "My wife's mother is seriously ill and we despair of her life."

When Jesus entered his house, He went immediately to her bedside and rebuked her high fever which threatened her life. To Simon's amazement, his mother-in-law not only arose, but she even appeared as if she had never been sick and began to serve Jesus and all her family as well. Of course the news of these things went abroad, and people began to throng to hear Jesus preach and teach. The synagogues in that area were full to overflowing. But people were not waiting for the Sabbath to hear Jesus. They followed Him wherever He went. One morning when Simon, his brother Andrew and the other fishermen had spent a disappointing night on the lake with nothing to show for their hard work, Jesus was there on the shore and hundreds of people were crowding around Him. Simon and the other fishermen had spread out their nets to dry. Jesus stepped into Simon's boat and asked him to push out a little ways so He could address the people who followed Him. When He had finished speaking to the crowds He said to Simon, "Put out into deep water and let down your nets for a catch." Peter responded, "Master, we fished all night and caught nothing, but if you say so I will let down my nets." Lo and behold, their nets were full to the breaking point. Simon and Andrew signaled to the other fishers to bring their boat and help them. They came and both boats were so filled they were in danger of sinking. Simon was overwhelmed with all he had seen and heard the last few days.

He heard preaching and teaching such as he had never heard before. He witnessed the healing of many people who were truly sick, including his own mother-in-law who had been brought back from the point of death. He had seen and heard Jesus expel demons; and now this: two boats filled and overflowing with fish that had not been there the night before. "Depart from me, Lord, for I am a sinful man," was Simon's response. Simon was convinced by all that he had seen and heard that Jesus was all that John the Baptist had said He was and more. It is only in the presence of God that people sense their own sinfulness. Dr. William Hendricksen, the noted commentator said in his commentary on the Gospel of Luke, "When one is confronted with Jesus, it is impossible to remain neutral. His enemies react to His miracles with hatred and reviling; His true disciples, with homage and reverence. They stoop and worship."

Yes, Simon had acknowledged Jesus as his Lord and Master. When Jesus responded to his humble words, "Depart from me, Lord, for I am a sinful man," He said to trembling Simon, "Fear not; from henceforth you will catch men." So after the boat returned to shore and the miraculous catch was sold, Simon Peter, his brother Andrew, and his business partners, John and James, sons of Zebedee, left everything and became disciples of Jesus, remaining with Him until He was arrested, tried and executed. They all heard the many sermons and lessons of Jesus. They all witnessed His amazing miracles. They were with Him when he fed five thousand men with a handful of bread and fish. Later He repeated this same kind of miracle He fed four thousand hungry people. They saw Him change water into wine, heal the sick and even raise the dead. They were in a sinking boat when Jesus calmed the storm and their fears. On another occasion, when they were caught on the lake in a wild storm without Jesus, they saw Him coming to them walking on the storm tossed waters. They all cried out in fear, thinking they had seen a ghost. But when Jesus assured them it was He, Simon called out, "Lord, if it is really You, allow me to come to You." Jesus bade him to come. Simon found himself walking on the waters too, until he took his eyes off Jesus and looked at the waves and felt the wind and began to sink. Jesus took his hand and brought him safely back to the boat—a much wetter, but wiser man.

As time went on, the disciples became more and more convinced that Jesus was indeed the promised Messiah; but they were also confused by some of the things Jesus was saying to them. They were also very disappointed that so many of their fellow countrymen rejected Him and His teaching and, furthermore, seemed to hate and resent Him. His preaching and teaching challenged the long held interpretation of the Old Testament. These traditions, many of which took all the true meaning of God's Word and turned it around from the original intention, were more highly and jealously regarded than the Word itself. Jesus exposed the shallow and false interpretations for what they were…the traditions of men. His teachings had about them the ring of truth and exposed the traditions of men as being out of accord with the will of God revealed in His holy word. This was unforgivable to the learned scribes and the Pharisees. So while His popularity with the common people increased greatly, the anger of the establishment became more and more intense and deadly.

As the time for Jesus' arrest and death drew nearer, He took His disciples aside; and they left Judah and Galilee and came into the Gentile area near the region of Caesarea Philippi. This area had been beautified by Philip the Tetrarch in honor of Caesar Augustus and was dedicated to one of Caesar's favorite gods, Pan. Jesus had deliberately chosen this place, removed from the arena of growing conflict with the Jewish authorities. There He might have a time of prayer and also time to prepare His disciples for the coming conflict with the religious leaders which would result in His condemnation and death.

So He began to question the disciples asking, "Whom do men say that I, the Son of Man am?" Their response omitted the angry and belittling opinion of the leaders, who went so far to say that Jesus was an agent of Satan. "Some say that You are John the Baptist, some Elijah; and others Jeremiah or one of the prophets." The interesting thing about these names was that each of them was regarded by many as a forerunner of the Messiah, not the Messiah Himself. Then He asked the far more important question for them and for us. "But you," He asked, "Who do you say that I am?" Simon's answer is the classic profession, required of all who would claim to be followers of Jesus. Notice that here is one of the few times in the synoptic Gospels (Matthew, Mark, and Luke) that this disciple is referred to as both Simon and Peter. There is a profound sense of solemnity in Matthew's report of this occasion.

Peter said, "You are the Christ, the Anointed One of God, the Son of the living God." Let all hear this who would say we must not refer to Jesus Christ as the Son of God lest the Muslims be offended. Let all hear this who say that Jesus was just a good man, nothing more. Jesus accepted Simon Peter's answer with delight, approval and commendation. In the final analysis any lesser profession is unacceptable, then and now.

Jesus' response to Simon Peter's confession was almost startling to him and all the other disciples. "Blessed are you Simon, son of John! For flesh and blood did not reveal this unto you, but My Father who is in heaven. And this I say unto you that you are Petros, (a piece of rock); and on this bedrock I will build My church, and over it the gates of hell shall not prevail." It is not the purpose of this book to delve into the full meaning of this profession of faith made by Simon Peter. Nor is it the purpose to deal with the Lord's answer to him which is the focal point of much controversy and even divisions in the church. But it is the purpose of this book to show the role Simon Peter had in the trial and death of Jesus of Nazareth.

However, a few things must be made clear in order to grasp the pivotal role this encounter played in our understanding of the whole drama of the killing of Jesus of Nazareth. Peter's confession was based upon his observation of the person and amazing ministry of Jesus. But as Jesus said in His response to Peter, this truth was revealed to him by the Father in heaven. The truth that Jesus was, and always will be, indeed the Christ, the Son of God, in the unique sense of the word, is the foundation of all Christian truth and thus the foundation of the church. Jesus' response must also be considered; especially the words, "You are Peter(rock) and upon this rock I will build My church." Jesus did not say to him, "You are

Peter and upon you I will build My church". Later developments help us understand what Jesus meant by these words that it was upon Peter, the confessor of Christ, along with the other apostles, Christ would build His church. In fact when Peter addressed the church in one of his final messages, 1 Peter 2:4-10, he referred to Jesus Christ as the cornerstone of the church and believers as the living stones being built up into a spiritual house. Truly, "The church's one foundation is Jesus Christ her Lord," but the Apostles were, in a secondary sense only, the foundation stones of the early church. It is obvious that Peter and the other apostles never thought of him as having a unique role in Christ's building of His church. The promise that they, the disciples, would be given the keys of the kingdom is directly related to their faithful stewardship of the word of God. Later, at the Jewish feast called Pentecost, Peter would proclaim the good news and three thousand hearts and lives were opened by the powerful keys of the Gospel applied by the Holy Spirit.

Peter seemed to have seriously misunderstood the implications of his own profession and the words of Christ. For when Jesus began to explain plainly the fact and necessity of His coming suffering and death in His role as "The Christ, the Son of the living God," Peter and all the disciples were horrified and dumbfounded. So Simon Peter took Jesus aside and began to rebuke Him, saying, "Far be it from You, Lord! This will never happen to you!" Peter was quite willing to believe and confess that Jesus was truly the Messiah, the Son of the Living God, but unwilling to believe or accept this meant suffering and death for Jesus. He had much yet to learn. Jesus' response to Simon Peter's rebuke cut deeply. "He turned and said to Simon Peter(the rock) "Get behind Me, Satan! You are a hindrance to me. For you are not seeking the things of God, but those of men." In this one encounter Simon Peter would

128

be praised as one to whom God revealed the precious truth of the saving Gospel. Then when Peter rebuked Jesus for mentioning His approaching death, he in turn was rebuked for being Satan's agent. There would be no escaping the cross for Jesus in His role as redeemer. And according to Jesus' own words, there is no escaping the cross of self-denial for those who follow Him. This, Peter would learn; and if church history and tradition are accurate, Peter himself would also be crucified.

As the hostility towards Jesus increased and the leaders of the people began to be more outspoken and aggressive in this opposition, the anxiety and fear of His disciples began to grow also. This would all come to a head as the time drew near for the annual Passover. Much to the consternation of Peter and all the disciples, Jesus seemed determined to be in Jerusalem for the occasion. They pled with Him not to go, but bravely announced their purpose to go with Him and to die also. Great crowds of people from Judea, Galilee, and everywhere else in the Roman Empire where colonies of Jewish people existed began to come to the Holy City for Passover. Jesus' reputation had been spread far and wide. One question in the minds of many people who came to the celebration was this; "Will Jesus dare to come to Jerusalem for Passover?" It was no secret that the establishment hated Him and wanted badly to eliminate Him and any who followed Him.

Jesus, knowing all this, and knowing what awaited Him, set his face steadfastly to go to Jerusalem and there fulfill the role assigned Him by the Father and so poignantly prophesied by Isaiah and the other prophets of old. He was not dissuaded by the pleas and protests of His disciples, Simon Peter among them. When Jesus entered Jerusalem, he did so in a manner to fulfill Scripture. He came not as a conquering hero arrayed for battle and mounted on a great war horse. Rather he came meekly riding on a donkey, a symbol of peace. This was in conscious fulfillment of the Prophet Zechariah's words of long ago. "Rejoice greatly, O daughter of Zion! Shout aloud, O daughter of Jerusalem! Behold your king is coming unto you; He is righteous and having salvation, humble and mounted on a donkey, even on a colt, the foal of a donkey."

Jesus was deliberately offering Himself to the nation as their true Messiah, their King of peace. The thronging pilgrims who were entering the city and many within the city gates greeted him with high hopes and joy. The leaders also caught on to what he was doing, and they intensified their efforts to arrest and destroy Him lest they would lose their own positions of authority and power. No doubt Peter and the rest of the disciples were filled with high hopes once more. Surely his words about suffering, rejection, condemnation and crucifixion were not to be taken literally. But those hopes were soon dashed. It became obvious that Jesus was determined to die. It was then that Simon Peter came to the firm conviction that come what may, he, alone if necessary, would stand by Jesus to the bitter end, even to prison or death. This he affirmed more than once and with steely determination to carry out his vow. So he bravely attempted to defend Jesus when he was arrested. He was facing not only temple guards, but Romans as well. Still he drew his sword and waded into the arresting mob, swinging his sword and prepared to die. In the darkness and confusion his blow went wide the mark and instead of decapitating the guard, he severed his ear. But he was not through. The next blow would be fatal, even the Roman guards shrank back from this angry giant of a man who defended Jesus. Just before he could rush forward and die fighting the enemies of Jesus, he heard the firm and stern order from Jesus; "Put away your sword, Peter, I will drink the bitter cup the Father has given Me!" At that word, Peter joined the other disciples and fled the scene.

He did not flee in panic, and he did not go far. And as he saw that John was closely following after Jesus and the arresters, he fell in with John, still determined to do what he could to save Jesus from His captors. As they hurried along trying to keep the mob and Jesus in sight, John may have whispered to Peter as they went: "It was Judas who brought them to the garden. He went up to Jesus and kissed him in order that the guards might seize the right man. How could he do such a thing?" Peter was shocked to hear this, for none of them thought Judas would be the one to betray Him. He thought to himself, "Judas will wish he had never been born when I get through with him." They were approaching the palace of the High Priest. Because John was known to him and apparently his servants too, he was allowed to enter the courtyard and took Peter with him. John even was allowed inside, but Peter had to wait outside; and it was a very chilly night. Someone started a first and all began to gather closer to it to stay warm. What courage Peter showed, what daring! With the exception of John, the rest had run away. Not Peter. He waited for some word. For he was still determined to stand by Jesus to the death. That's when it all started. Some of those standing out there thought they recognized Peter and began accusing him and baiting him. When Peter answered gruffly that he was not one of the disciples of Jesus, they could tell from his accent he was a Galilean; and their taunting increased. The rest of this sad story has already been recounted earlier in this chapter. Yes, he actually denied even knowing who Jesus was; and being angry his words were bitter curses and hot denials. Then Jesus came out in time to hear him, and from afar came the crowing of a rooster. He still loved Jesus, but surrounded by the darkness, helpless to do anything to rescue his Lord, and taunted by those in the garden, his courage failed him; and he fled weeping into the darkness, leaving Jesus to face a much greater darkness alone and friendless.

Battle of Gethsemane

Much of the history of the human race is defined by crucial battles fought and won…or lost. There were many such battles recorded in the ancient world, and some of these became turning points in the history of the human race. In more relatively recent history we might point to the battle of Waterloo, a small town in Belgium in which the Emperor Napoleon was defeated by the Allied armies and his dream of reclaiming his lost empire was forever lost. The battle of Gettysburg in the War Between the States in our own country was the high water of the Confederate's dream of a new nation and the beginning of the end that came 18 months later. We could go on and on recalling famous battles and the history making and changing results that followed. There was the Battle of Stalingrad on the eastern front of World War 2 and the Battle of the Bulge on the western front of that same war, which were very strategic in the war's outcome.

There is another famous battle that occurred with much higher stakes for the world and for all those who look to Jesus of Nazareth as Savior and Lord. This battle was not fought on a raging battle-field with flags flying, drums beating, or cannons thundering. It did not involve massive armies clashing with appalling casualties. In fact it is never mentioned or even considered to be a battle in the minds of most. It is seldom, if ever, mentioned except by those who go through a strange and seemingly futile ceremony (in the eyes of the world) of eating a mere bite of bread and sipping just a taste of the fruit of the vine. In that ceremony they talk about what happened in a small garden they call Gethsemane. They note well that He won that battle, yet the next day, as a result of His victory, He suffered a terrible death.

Jesus of Nazareth had finished His earthly ministry except for the one great thing He had come into the world to be and to do... "The Lamb of God who takes away the sin of the world." He well knew what was coming. He had warned His disciples what He and they would face as He made his way from the Passover feast to the lonely place where this battle would be fought. Knowing that the Traitor would soon be coming and with him the arresting guards, He left some of His disciples just within the scope of the small garden and took with Him the inner circle of His most trusted followers, Peter, James and John into the deeper recesses of the garden. He asked them to watch and pray with Him. But even these most trusted friends, overcome with fatigue and fear, fell asleep and left Him alone, bereft of any earthly comfort or comforter. There in the darkness of the little hidden garden, and the greater darkness of His own grief and deep distress, the Battle of Gethsemane was joined. The outcome of this battle would determine the issues of life and death for countless millions. His defeat would mean the triumph of evil, of darkness over light, death over life, and hate over love. His victory would make possible a glorious kingdom, a renewed and restored creation, and a victory whose consequences would endure forever and ever.

After Jesus took Peter, James and John aside, He began to be filled with sorrow and anguish. He had promised His disciples victory over the world and bequeathed to them peace, His peace; little did they know the dreadful price He would pay, the travail of soul He would endure to make this peace possible for them. And it all began at the battle of Gethsemane. He said to these three, "My soul is overwhelmed with sorrow, even to the point of death; stay here, watch and pray with Me, lest you enter into temptation." Jesus went a little farther and kneeled down, then fell on His face and the battle was joined in earnest. No doubt He was tempted to pray, "Father deliver me from this hour;" but it was for this hour He had come into the world and He knew He had to face it. He also knew that if He won this victory, a greater sorrow would come upon Him the next day.

What was this "greater sorrow," this terrible thing from which, if possible, He would turn away? Was it that He knew Judas, His professed friend, would soon lead the arresting officer to take Him? Was it because there, near at hand were His three best friends too weary to stay awake with Him and pray? Was it the dreadful ordeal of the trial and the greater ordeal of the physical suffering He would endure on the Roman cross while being taunted and mocked by His enemies? Who would not shrink from such suffering and shame? All of this was involved, but the real ordeal would be when His soul was made an offering for sin, all the sins for all those whom the Father had given Him. In commenting on this incredible sacrifice, the Apostle Paul would later say, "He(God) made Him (Jesus) to be sin for us that we might become the righteousness of God through Him." William Hendricksen asked, "Did He, perhaps, here in Gethsemane see this tidal wave of God's wrath because of our sin, coming?" This was the real, the true battle, that all our sin would be laid to His charge; and He would therefore pay the price when He took our place before the Holy Father.

Jesus certainly wanted His three good friends near Him as He went through this awful ordeal, but they could not go through it with

Him. It was His burden, and His alone, for no mere mortal could share the depths with the Son of God who alone was "without spot and blemish." This was why He came, but now the hour had come when He must either turn back from His mission or determine that He would fulfill it even at the unthinkable price He must pay. So falling on His face, He cried out from the depths of His being, "O My Father, if it is possible let this cup pass from me; nevertheless, not as I will, but as You will." Jesus knew that if He took the place of sinners, He must pay the debt they owe. He well knew there was no other way, yet he would have His disciples and all His people for all times know this too. If there had been another way, why would the Loving Father, who had declared by His own voice, "This is My beloved Son, in whom I am well pleased" withhold that "other way"?

Did Jesus not know this was the only way? Of course He knew, but He also knew that fallen human nature would think there were many ways to handle the sin problem. The sleepy disciples may have heard His prayer, or after His resurrection He may have told them of His ordeal in the garden. Either way it was so important that they understood this great truth, that He bore the unbearable, for there was no other way. It is also important for all to realize this same truth. Why look for another way when Jesus told His disciples before He entered Gethsemane, "I am the way, the truth and the life"? If there was another way, would not the Father who loved His Son from all eternity have provided it? There is deep mystery in these things, but even more marvelous grace and goodness. The sacrifice Jesus made when He prayed, "…Not My will, but Your will, Father, be done" is beyond understanding, but not beyond simple faith. In the words of an old hymn, "Jesus paid it all, all to Him I owe," is the heart-song of all believers. That debt of gratitude is not limited to what happened at the Battle of Gethsemane, but surely that battle is a large part of it.

When Jesus returned to the three men whom He had exhorted to stay awake, he found them asleep. They were understandably weary, for the hour was very late, and their hearts were heavy. Jesus said to Peter, who had proclaimed his undying loyalty, "Simon, are you asleep?" And to him and the two others He said, "Watch and pray that you may not enter in to temptation. The spirit indeed is willing, but the flesh is weak." I think this was a warning to stay awake spiritually because they were soon to be assailed with severe temptation. This timely warning was for these men Jesus loved and for all for whom He would soon die. Our good intentions are not always matched by our actions.

Again, a second time, Jesus went back to His lonely vigil and continued to earnestly pray. Though He had surrendered to the Father's will, the battle was not yet done. The horror of what He would face was almost overwhelming. Still He prayed saying, "My Father if You are willing take this cup away from me: nevertheless if this cannot pass from me unless I drink it, not My will, but Your will be done." Willing to do the Father's will and "drink the cup" was His commitment, but still He asked the Father to remove the cup from Him. The Father's answer was to send a consoling An-gel to strengthen Him in His resolve. The willing Son was, how-ever, in deep agony. For the dark cloud of all the sins of a fallen race was overwhelming. The realization that the Father must deal with His Beloved Son as if He were the worst of sinners and rebels brought Jesus to the brink of utter despair. The physical agony of this cosmic struggle caused Jesus to break out in sweat mingled with blood. The comforting Angel was not sent to tell Him the cup had been removed, but to give Him strength to endure it. It is impossible to fully understand what Jesus was going through, but extreme anguish, deep supplication, fearful anticipation were all combined to bring Him to the brink of despair and even close to death. All this and the greater horror of the cross facing Jesus the next day was because He loved those whom the Father had given Him. "Greater love has no one than this, that one should lay down his life for his friends," He had said to His disciples. Truly He would pay this price in full measure not only in the battle of Gethsemane, but even more in the great darkness of the cross.

The traitor along with the soldiers and temple guards would soon arrive there, but now for the third time Jesus went before the Father and prayed as he had been praying. For the third and last time Jesus asked the Father to remove the dreaded cup. For the third time He also surrendered to the inevitable result of His loving acceptance of the Father's will that all who ever would look to Him for salvation and life would find it.

The battle of Gethsemane was won and the Victor would soon die in agony and pain on a Roman cross.

10

Arrest in the Garden

The Battle of Gethsemane had been won. The war was about to begin. After Jesus had completed His prayer to the Father the third time, He awakened his disciples and told them "The hour has come, and the Son of man is betrayed into the hands of sinners. Rise let us be going. Lo, My betrayer is at hand!" At this point a "great crowd" drew near, and Judas, one of the twelve (disciples) was leading them.

Who was in this "great crowd"? Judas, of course, led the way, and he was followed by a mixed multitude. Included were temple guards and servants of the High Priest, probably members of the Sanhedrin, certain scribes and Levites, and last of all a cohort of Roman Legionaries. The latter was probably less than an entire cohort of six hundred men, but a considerable number nonetheless. The large numbers and especially the presence of Roman soldiers would indicate that the authorities were concerned lest there might be a large number of people with Jesus prepared to defend Him. They knew thousands of pilgrims had come to the city for the Passover celebration, and many of these might well be followers of the Galilean and prepared to take His side in any conflict. So the arresting mob was sent in the dead of night, and their numbers were large just in case of resistance. They also bore with them many swords, clubs and torches.

The eleven disciples had been awakened in the middle of the night by Jesus' words of warning, but also by the noise and lights. They were fearful, confused and huddled together not sure what they were supposed to do. Perhaps for a moment they were reassured for there was Judas greeting Jesus with friendly words and a kiss of greeting. Any doubt about the intention of Judas was resolved when they heard Jesus say, "Judas, are you betraying the Son of Man with a kiss?" Then as if to show Judas how futile and unnecessary his betrayal was, Jesus stepped forward and faced the crowd. "Whom are you seeking?" He asked. "Jesus of Nazareth", they replied. "I am He, Jesus responded. The effect was wholly unexpected. Those in front of the mob drew back and fell to the ground! How do we explain this action? Was it merely surprise that He would so readily identify Himself? Or was there more to this? Consider this: they had been sent on what was thought to be a dangerous mission. There might be hundreds, if not thousands who would rally to the Galilean's side. Word had spread far and wide about His miraculous powers. The leaders who sent them on this quest had publicly stated that Jesus was in league with Satan, and His great power arose from this connection. All had heard about His raising of a man who had been dead four days. There was no telling what He might do to anyone who laid hands on Him. Given all this and the unexpected nature of Jesus' self-identification they began to back away and in the darkness fell over each other.

There is another thing to consider. Not too long before His arrest Jesus had told His disciples, "I lay down My life for the sheep. No one takes it away from Me, I lay it down on My own initiative. I have authority to lay it down, and I have authority to take it up again. This charge I have received from the Father." It may well be that the fear of the mob and their failure on their first attempt to seize Jesus was a momentary demonstration of the truth that Jesus voluntarily submitted to this arrest. Jesus never used His authority and power to care for Himself but only to minister to others. This could well be the real reason the angry, determined mob found itself helpless to seize Jesus.

Again Jesus asked the confused and frightened mob, "Whom do you seek?" They said again, "Jesus of Nazareth." Jesus answered, "I told you that I am He." "If you are therefore seeking me," and pointing to His disciples He said, "Let these go away." Knowing why He had come into the world, and having been assured once more of His mission on earth as He prayed in Gethsemane, Jesus gave Himself over to the will and fury of His enemies. To the credit of Jesus' disciples and especially to Peter, they were ready at Jesus' word to resist the arrest, even to the point of risking their lives to do so. Peter bravely faced the overwhelming numbers of the band sent to arrest Jesus, even knowing there were trained and seasoned Roman soldiers reinforcing the temple guard. He was ready to live up to his sworn word to Jesus that he would never forsake Him even if it meant his death! So taking one of the two swords the disciples had with them, Peter leaped into action. If he had to die defending Jesus he was prepared to do just that. In the darkness his aim at the temple guard who had dared to lay his miserable hands on Jesus went awry so instead of decapitating him, Peter only severed his ear. But Jesus rebuked Peter saying, "Put away your sword! For all who live by the sword will die by the sword. Don't you understand that even now I could call to My Father and He would send twelve full armies of Angels? How then would the Scriptures be fulfilled that it must be so? The cup which the Father has given me, shall I not drink it?" With those words Jesus, in effect, disarmed Peter and at the same time reached out and healed the stricken servant. Confused and frightened, and forbidden to defend Him, Peter and the other ten disciples simply fled away.

Who could blame them? Jesus would indeed fully and beautifully forgive them, and especially boastful Peter, and only because of this would Peter ever be able to forgive himself. But not yet, this would come later after Jesus would have made forgiveness possible not only for Peter but for all who would ever seek it and find it.

Now Jesus was left alone to face not only the arresting mob, but that which lay ahead for Him at His trials and His execution. Jesus then faced the arresters, even the chief priests, elders, temple guards and the Roman soldiers and said: "Have you come out against me with swords and clubs as if I were a robber?" He asked. "Daily I was with you teaching in the temple and you did not arrest Me nor attempt to restrain Me. But this has all come to pass to fulfill what the prophets have written. This is your hour and the power of darkness." Isn't it ironic that those who accused Jesus of doing His mighty works by the power of Satan, now placed themselves, these holy men, at Satan's disposal to do his bidding?

The fleeing disciples made good their escape. One young man barely made it by leaving behind his clothing as he ran away. Led by the Roman soldiers and the officers of the Sanhedrin, Jesus was roughly bound and led away to trial. The end(or so they thought) was now in sight, and this trouble maker would be killed and all his followers dispersed forever (or so they thought).

11

The First Hearing and Trial

The first step in the killing of Jesus of Nazareth was now taken-He was under arrest. Next He was taken to the home of Annas, the former High Priest and father-in-law of the reigning High Priest Caiaphas. There He was questioned by this man, Annas, the real power behind the throne of his son-in-law. We are not told why He was taken first to Annas, but we may recognize that Annas was the first to officially (yet unofficially) question Jesus. Probably Annas wished to be able to send Jesus to Caiaphas, the ruling High Priest, with a charge that would result in the death penalty. Or perhaps this was an effort on the part of Annas to simply show his son-in-law Caiaphas who was really in charge. We are not told enough about this relationship between these two conniving men to know exactly how things stood between them or why Jesus was taken before Annas first.

The interview was relatively brief and inconclusive and was out of accord with Jewish law and custom of the time. Annas, of all men, would know this but it soon became obvious that neither he, Caiaphas, nor any of the others were concerned with the legal details of what was happening. Their one aim was to condemn Jesus to death and pressure the Roman governor to acquiesce to their demands. As the old man, Annas, looked at the young man Jesus, who knows what thoughts passed his mind? That He was intelligent Annas well knew, for He had confounded every effort of the best minds in the nation to trap Him and trip Him. His knowledge of the law was wide and deep, but He was constantly pointing out that many of the traditions of Judaism were opposed to the Law of Moses rather than explaining those laws.

The one great unforgivable, however, was the threat He posed to the lucrative business associated with the temple worship. He had twice denounced this trafficking and had even physically overturned the tables of the money changers and the sellers of animals for the sacrificial rites of the temple. Then He literally drove them out of the temple with whips and thongs. He verbally assaulted that whole system as profaning the temple and changing it from a house of prayer for all nations to a den of robbers! How dare He speak so? By what authority did He do these things. When asked about His authority He evaded the questions and tried to change the subject by asking them about the Baptism of John the Baptist. All the elite of Judaism knew that John was a mad man, but the common people still thought he was a great Prophet, so the leaders dared not speak against John. Now this man who claimed to be the Messiah, the Son of God, had cleverly dodged the issue of authority. But he would soon find out who was the real authority and how puny His claims were.

Annas began the questioning by asking Jesus who His disciples were and also questioned Him about His teaching. Jesus ignored the question about His disciples. He knew they were known and had been closely watched for many months. He had already asked the arresting officers in the garden to let His disciples go since they had Him in custody. In order to further protect them, Jesus began to answer Annas' second line of questioning about His teachings.

144

He said, "I spoke openly to the world: always I taught in the synagogues and in the temple, where all the Jews assemble, and I said nothing in secret. Why do you question me? Question those who have heard me as to what I said to them; behold they know what I said."

When Jesus had said these things, one of the temple guards, an officer, struck Jesus in the face saying, "Do you answer the High Priest this way?" Jesus responded, "If I spoke wrongly, then bear witness of the wrong; but if rightly why do you strike me?" They both knew, as well as Annas, that this striking was against the law and should have resulted in Annas rebuking the guard or even disqualifying him from bearing witness against Jesus later in the formal trial. Annas and the guard, and indeed all those who took part in the arrest and trial of Jesus of Nazareth, would soon enough stand trial before a just and holy Judge who would hold them accountable for what they had said and done. The sentence of that court would be righteous and irrevocable.

Annas then sent Jesus away to Caiaphas, still bound and by now bearing the first marks of brutality on His wrists and in His face. As Jesus turned to leave and go to the trial before the High Priest, which would result in His condemnation and execution, He heard a loud voice protesting that he was not a disciple of this man, nor did he even know Him at all. That loud voice, of course, belonged to Jesus' best friend, Simon Peter. This was the same man who earlier in this same evening had protested that he would never deny Jesus, even if it meant prison or death. This man Peter had made a solemn vow, and now with an unholy oath, he broke that sacred vow. This was the last time these two friends would look on each other until the third day after Jesus died.

The night was growing late, and the dawn was not too far off when Jesus was brought before the High Priest Caiaphas and the hastily assembled Jewish high court, the Sanhedrin. Though the law strictly forbade that such a trial be held at night, Caiaphas proceeded with the trial in spite of that restriction, and there was no objection. Jewish law also required that a verdict could not be reached in a capital case on the same day in which the evidence was heard. That requirement, too, was ignored. Witnesses had been heard, but it became obvious that these witnesses were contradicting each other and even themselves. Still, more witnesses were called in hope that some credible evidence might be heard to give the trial at least some semblance of legality. At last two more witnesses came forward with the accusation that Jesus had said, "I will destroy this temple of God that is made with hands, and in three days I will build another not made with hands." These two unnamed witnesses were misquoting what Jesus had said and perverted it to make it sound worse. What Jesus had said almost three years before this improper trial was, "Destroy this temple, and in three days I will raise it up." Those words were spoken when Jesus had driven the merchants and the money changers out of the temple at the first Passover He attended after He began His public ministry. Still, these two witnesses, contradicted each other. Even if they had not, the charge would certainly not be considered blasphemy. Caiaphas knew that if that was all they had to present to Pilate to secure a death sentence, he would dismiss them with deserved scorn.

It was not as if the Sanhedrin was considering charges against Jesus of Nazareth for the first time. Apparently this august body had talked of little else for many months. They were deeply concerned and alarmed at the mounting flood of popularity Jesus was receiving. They no longer even attempted to deny His many miracles. The greatest and latest had been the raising of Lazarus from the grave four days after his death. Too many people had witnessed this amazing event. They did not even attempt to deny it. Certainly it was the immediate reason Jesus had been welcomed into

Jerusalem with such wide spread and joyful acclaim. It was also the reason for a hastily called and frantic meeting of the council to determine how to deal with the Galilean. It was at that meeting Caiaphas persuaded the whole council the only solution would be the execution of Jesus. From that day on they plotted to put Him to death and sought ways to bring about His execution.

Now at last they had him! The arrest away from the city and at night had been arranged very well. Now if they could just proceed with their plans, He would be well disposed of before many people knew what was happening. The fact that his close disciples had fled in frantic flight was another unexpected, but well planned, coup. But now their plans were being thwarted by Jesus' refusal to respond to their questions, and by the failure of the quickly assembled witnesses to come up with a coherent set of accusations which would form the basis for a guilty verdict and would merit the consent of the Roman governor.

Caiaphas and his cohorts were on the verge of being frustrated by Jesus' silence and refusal to defend Himself. With mounting fury and despair Caiaphas approached Jesus, unable to disguise his anger. "Do you answer nothing? Have you nothing to say about all these serious charges which have been brought against you?" He saw his case against Jesus in danger of falling apart. Even these biased judges would hesitate to so blatantly disregard the requirements of their laws, as much as they feared and hated Jesus. "This must not happen," he thought. All his carefully laid and crafty plans were beginning to crumble before his very face.

In desperation and in great anger, he stood before Jesus to make one last attempt to bring about a verdict of guilt and death against Jesus. What an ironic contrast between the two, Jesus and Caiaphas. Jesus was dressed in his simple clothing and covered with a seamless, woven robe. By this time His face would have been swollen and bloody. His wrists were lacerated by the bonds He had now worn for hours. His fatigue would be obvious. He had spoken no words through all the insistent questioning. No doubt his countenance was sad but somehow serene. He had already made His heart-wrenching decision to drink the cup the Father had given Him, even to the last bitter and painful dregs. Caiaphas, on the other hand, was arrayed in the impressive garments befitting his lofty office as God's High Priest. He had no doubt presided over the killing of many Passover lambs in his role. He would have never used the words, but he was determined there was one more Lamb which must be slain.

Standing before him was the one of whom he had spoken scarcely more than one week before. At that time the Sanhedrin had assembled to discuss and plan how to respond to the undeniable miracle of the raising of Lazarus from the dead. "What shall we do with this man who has performed so many miraculous signs? If we let him alone, everyone will believe in Him, and the Romans will come and take away our own positions of authority and power and even our liberty and identity as a nation." The response of Caiaphas revealed his own cynicism and moral corruption. "You understand nothing! This man must die or else our whole nation will perish, and we with it."

He simply was not going to be deterred in his determination to have Jesus put to death! It was both expedient and absolutely necessary for Jesus to die. His anger had reached the boiling point. How dare this pretender, this self-proclaimed Messiah, this nobody, put Caiaphas and the whole system he represented at risk. His eyes ablaze, his temper at fever pitch, he screamed into the face of Jesus with almost maniacal fury and desperation, " Are you the

Messiah, the Son of the blessed? In the name of the one true living God, I demand that you tell us if you are the Son of God."

Jesus knew exactly what Caiaphas was doing, seeking to make Him condemn himself in the eyes of the Sanhedrin. He also knew that continued silence was His right before the judges according to Jewish law. Then Jesus boldly and bravely answered this direct question with a direct answer by which He affirmed again what He had always claimed, "It is as you have said...I AM! And I warn you all hereafter, you will see the Son of Man, enthroned at the right hand of the Almighty One, and returning upon the clouds of heaven."

At those words, Caiaphas knew Jesus had condemned Himself, but he also knew he must show great shock and righteous indignation. So tearing his clothes as an expression of holy wrath, and turning to face the shocked men of the Sanhedrin, Caiaphas cried out in triumph, "He has blasphemed! Why do we need any other witnesses? You yourselves have heard Him speak this blasphemy. What do you think?"

They all in great anger answered back, "He deserves to be put to death!" It was not necessary to follow the correct procedure of polling each member—they all were in spontaneous agreement, He must die! They must wait until the Council could be officially convened at daybreak, for no official action could be taken at night. So while they awaited the approaching hour, these dignified and holy judges crowded around Jesus and began to assault Him by spitting in His face. Others lost complete control of themselves and began to pound Jesus in His face. The guards who were holding Him mocked Him and blindfolded Him. Then they too began to strike His face saying, "Prophesy! Prophesy to us you 'Messiah'! Tell us, who struck you?" They cursed Him, and they who condemned Jesus for blasphemy spoke great blasphemy against Him. Thus, "He was oppressed and He was afflicted, yet He opened not His mouth. He was led as a lamb to the slaughter, and as a sheep before its shearers is silent, so He opened not His mouth"

"Then immediately when it was day, all the elders of the people came together, both the chief priests and the scribes and held a consultation against Jesus to put Him to death." When the whole Sanhedrin was officially convened they turned on Jesus again saying, "If you are indeed the Messiah, tell us, the rulers of the people, are you the true Messiah? Answer us here and now!"

He responded, "if I tell you, you will not at all believe; and if I make inquiry you would not answer Me or let Me go." Then He added with grave solemnity, and I think with great pity, "Hereafter will the Son of Man be seated at the right hand of the power of God." They were shocked and indignant at the implication. He was saying, in effect, "I am on trial before you now, but at the final trial of all people, you will be on trial before Me, and I will have all authority and power as God Himself!"

Just to make sure they had heard Him correctly and to make His words the official admission of guilt, they posed the questions again, "So You are the Son of God?"

His answer stunned and angered them beyond all measure. "Yes, just as you say, I AM." They could scarcely believe what they had heard. He was saying of Himself what the living God had said of Himself when Moses had pled with Him, "Tell me Your name." They all agreed the trial was over. "We have heard with our own ears what he said with His own mouth. Bind Him and deliver Him to the hands of the Roman governor, Pontius Pilate, and require him to crucify this blasphemer!"

150

Unknown to the council, a man called Judas heard Jesus' words, knew for certainty they were true. He also heard the Council's verdict of death. It was too much. The horror of what he had done overwhelmed him, and he sought atonement-- not in the death Jesus had foretold many times, but in the futility of his own death by his own hands.

12

The Trial before Pontius Pilate

After the Jewish Sanhedrin men had reached their verdict of blasphemy, the next move would be to seek permission from the Roman Governor, Pontius Pilate for the death penalty for Jesus. Pontius Pilate, governor of Judea by the grace of Caesar Tiberius, had been serving in that capacity for several years when word reached him that the Jewish court had sentenced a young traveling Rabbi named Jesus of Nazareth to death, and were seeking his approval for death by crucifixion. Three malefactors who had been tried and convicted by Pilate were also awaiting execution.

Though Pilate was the supreme ruler of the province of Judea, he was not totally secure in his present position as governor. He was well aware that the Jews resented and hated him and were constantly seeking his removal. He hated and despised the Jews and had no sympathy at all for their desire to be a free republic. He was also aware that Tiberius was unpredictable and given to bouts of paranoia and resulting rage which he might take out on any in his administration who caused him trouble. Complaints about Pilate had already been sent to Tiberius earlier, and this only served to increase his hatred of the Jewish leaders, and at the same time, his reluctance to antagonize them further.

That was the situation when he received the request from Caiaphas for the confirmation of the death sentence for Jesus of Nazareth and His execution before the coming Sabbath which would begin at sundown this same day. It was still very early in the morning. The official Jewish trial of Jesus, which was held at daybreak, could have lasted no more than just a few minutes. Of course those bringing the message from the Sanhedrin could not enter the governor's residence, because according to the law and custom of that time and place this would have ceremonially defiled them. Thus it would have been impossible for them to eat the Passover meal. How ironic for these men to be so concerned about ceremonial uncleanness, when they had made themselves so morally and spiritually defiled by their actions in the trial of Jesus.

How do we explain the apparent contradiction that the Passover meal was eaten on the night before? That was the traditional time for the eating of the meal. Dr William Hendriksen offers the most plausible solution by referring to an earlier article written by one Dr. H. Mulder. "The text simply means that the members of the Sanhedrin had been so thoroughly pre-occupied with the arrest and trial of Jesus that they had not had time for their Passover meal. Thursday evening these mean had been awaiting Judas with his treachery. They did not know when he would come. The Sanhedrists had to be ready. They also wanted to take part as observers in the arrest. Then there was the night trial. All this took time, much time. Hence they were convinced that in the interest of the one really import assignment, namely to get rid of Jesus...all else, even the Passover supper could afford to wait. Hence when very early in the morning they brought Jesus before Pilate, they had not yet partaken of the Passover meal. They must not defile themselves by entering the house of a heathen. So these hypocrites who regarded ceremonial defilement to be so much worse than moral defilement could not enter the Praetorium. Once Jesus was actually hanging on a cross (mocked by them) they could then go home and eat the Passover lamb!"

So these holy men sent Jesus to Governor Pilate for the quick confirmation of the death sentence with the request that it be carried out before the Sabbath would begin at sundown this very same day. So this proud, sometimes cruel, and even superstitious man went out to receive and hear the Sanhedrin's minions. He addressed them with ill concealed contempt. "What accusations do you bring against this man?" Their response, "If he were not an evil doer, we would not have delivered him up to you," must have irritated proud Pilate. They, the messengers from the Sanhedrin, seemed to be saying to Pilate, "Your job is simply to agree with us and sentence Jesus to death." Pilate's response was also short and brusque. "Then you take him and judge him according to your own law." Their response was brief and straight to the point; "We are not permitted to put anyone to death." Pilate had won a small victory in making them acknowledge that he was indeed the final authority, nor could they ignore him or treat him with the contempt they had implied towards him.

Before this trial was over, Pilate himself would be faced with a threat that he would be accused of being "no friend of Caesar." This could end his career and his life and he knew it. However, at this point in the trial, the messengers from the Sanhedrin were only interested in one thing-to persuade Pilate to confirm the conviction and have Jesus crucified. So they began to enlarge on the crimes of Jesus by saying, "We found this fellow perverting the nation and forbidding to give tribute to Caesar, saying that he Himself is Messiah, a king." Not only this, but they began to enlarge on their charges going beyond what they had been told to say against Jesus.

Jesus' response surprised Pilate, for He answered not a word. Pilate said, "Do you answer nothing? Do you not hear how many things they are charging against you? Still, Jesus answered nothing even to one of the charges brought against Him. Pilate was amazed and baffled. Usually such a prisoner would be hotly denying all charges and pleading for his life, but not Jesus.

Perplexed, Pilate returned to the place of judgment, where the accusers dared not go lest they be defiled. Pilate wanted to question Jesus alone and not in the presence of His accusers. Pilate asked Jesus directly, "Are you the king of the Jews?" He assumed that Jesus, in the privacy of the judgment hall, would either deny the charge, or else would admit that He was truly the king of the Jews. Either way, Pilate would have the upper hand. What Pilate could not expect was the way in which Jesus answered his question, which would complicate matters even more.

Jesus first answered Pilate's question by asking him a question (which Jesus had frequently done during the last three years of public ministry). "Do you ask this of yourself, or did others say this of Me?"

Pilate's sharp reply was an indication his exasperation with this whole matter. "Am I a Jew? Your own nation and the religious leaders have given you over to me. What have you done?" He asked. Jesus' reply was even more perplexing to Pilate. "My kingdom is not of this world. If my kingdom were of this world, my servants would fight, that I might not be delivered up. (Remember, Jesus could have asked the Father, and He would have sent twelve armies of mighty angels, against which neither all the power of the Sanhedrin nor indeed the whole Roman Empire would have prevailed.) But my kingdom is not of this world."

So Pilate, intrigued by the words of Jesus said to Him, You are therefore a king?" Jesus answered him more fully. "It is as you say, I am a King; for this I was born. And for this I came into the world; that I should bear witness to the truth. Everyone who is of the truth heeds my voice." "But what is truth?" was Pilate's sardonic response.

He then went out to speak to the Jews, the priests and the gathering crowds; "I find no guilt in this man." That was not what they were prepared to hear. Time was getting away and still there was no confirmation of the death sentence they so fervently desired. So once more they began to reiterate and enlarge on their accusations. "He is stirring up the people, teaching throughout all Judea, starting in Galilee and even to this place." By those words, they unknowingly opened an escape route for Pilate to transfer the case to Herod since Jesus was from Galilee which was in Herod's jurisdiction. Besides by honoring Herod he would repair a breach between the two rulers, and enlist an ally in his never ending contests with the Jewish leaders. Herod would have been in Jerusalem for the Passover, so Jesus could be sent to him in a matter of a few minutes.

But Herod fared no better than Pilate in getting Jesus to answer his questions or even perhaps to see Him perform some remarkable miracle. The delegation from the Sanhedrin had followed Jesus and the guards to Herod and they heaped all sorts of accusations against Him but He answered them nothing. Herod took it all as a matter of jest and ridicule and dressed Jesus in gaudy apparel, mocked Him, and sent Him back to Pilate to handle.

Pilate realized that he could not escape the responsibility of hearing the case against Jesus and making a decision. From the words he spoke all through the process, we know that Pilate was convinced Jesus was innocent of the charges and said so at least three times. When Herod sent Jesus back to Pilate, he called together the priests and rulers of the people and said, "You brought me this man as one who was stirring up subversion; but on examining Him I found this man has no guilt at all in the things of which you have accused Him. Herod agreed with me and sent Him back to me. Listen, this man has done nothing worthy of death. You have a custom that I should release to you one man at the Passover. I will therefore scourge Him and release Him." The custom of pardoning one prisoner at that time was well established and was regarded as a "right" by the people. At this time there were at least three such prisoners, the most prominent of whom was Barabbas. This man was a robber, an insurrectionist and a murderer. He was under the sentence of death and was probably to be executed this very day. The multitude of the people began to clamor for Pilate to follow through with the custom and release one prisoner. Pilate saw his opportunity to release Jesus. Thinking they would prefer a man whom he, Pilate, had pronounced innocent, he offered them a choice; an innocent man who was the epitome of goodness, or a proven murderer. Pilate well knew it was from jealousy and envy the chief priests had sought His condemnation and death.

During this deliberation, Pilate's wife, who had conspired with others to get Pilate this appointment as Governor, sent word to him; "Do nothing to this righteous man for I have suffered many things in a dream because of him."

Pilate, who was a very superstitious man, took the warning seriously. But while he hesitated, the chief priests and elders of the people had done their work well. Undoubtedly they had bribed an unruly mob with promises and coins to demand Pilate to release

Barabbas instead of Jesus. The clamor and din increased as Pilate offered them a choice between Jesus and Barabbas, obviously favoring Jesus. But they cried out louder and louder, "Not this man, but Barabbas. Away with Jesus." Still desiring to release Jesus, Pilate answered back, "But what shall I do with Jesus whom you call 'King of the Jews?" They joined together, goaded on by the enemies of Jesus, and shouted again and again. "Let Him be crucified. Crucify, crucify Him! Still protesting Pilate said back to them, "Why? What evil has he done? I found in Him no guilt worthy of death. I shall scourge Him and release Him."

Pilate promptly ordered Jesus whipped with the dreaded Roman weapon of torture and punishment. The soldiers ordered to administer this terrible punishment, under which some prisoners had perished, thought they would have some fun with this man called "King of the Jews." So they made Him a crown of thorns and crammed it on His head. Somewhere they found a purple robe and wrapped it around Him. Then they began dancing around Him saying, Hail King of the Jews and striking Him with many hard blows to His head and face. Did Pilate dare think that the miserable and pitiful sight of Jesus so abused, would soften the attitude of the mob howling for His death? If so, he was sadly mistaken. Rather, their blood lust was raised to a fever pitch.

When Pilate cried out, "Behold the man," their response was an even more urgent and compelling demand to crucify Jesus. Beginning to see the futility of his attempt to release Jesus Pilate said with resignation but disgust, "You take Him and crucify Him, I find no guilt in Him."

The response of the Jewish leaders terrified Pilate. "We have a law, and by our law He ought to die, because He made Himself the

159

Son of God!" Pilate went immediately back into the judgment hall where Jesus was being held. He called Jesus back into his presence and said to Him, "Who are you and where are You from?" Jesus remained silent. Pilate said to Him, "You are not answering me? Don't you know that I have the authority to crucify you—or the authority to release You?

Jesus responded at last by saying, "You would have no authority over Me at all, were it not given you from above. Because of this those who delivered Me up to you have the greater sin." Terrified, torn Pilate kept trying to persuade the Jewish leaders that he wanted to release this strange man. But they were so determined to kill Jesus they knew what to say to insure His death. "If you release this man you are not a friend of Caesar. Anyone who makes himself out to be the king is speaking against Caesar."

Superstitious and frightened though he might have been, he was also a realist. The fear of offending Caesar even outweighed the possibility of offending some sort of God. But Pilate, too, had one last card to play—that the throngs of people outside might demand the release of Jesus. He was to be bitterly disappointed. When he took Jesus outside, he cried out, "Behold your king!" The high priests had done their work well among the rabble. They had bribed the right people to do their bidding. Instead of insisting on Jesus' release, they cried out again and again, "Away with Him! Away with Him! Crucify Him! Pilate tried one more time; "Shall I crucify your king?" The High Priest led the chant over and over again, "We have no king but Caesar."

To avoid the building riot, Pilate finally caved in to their demands. But in order that all might know (or so he hoped) that he himself was innocent of the blood of this righteous man, Pilate took water and washed his hands before them all saying, "I am innocent of the blood of this good man." So he released Barabbas and delivered Jesus up to their wrath.

We know what happened to Jesus, but what happened to Pilate after this? The information is sketchy at best. We do know that in less than two years after this trial he was recalled by Caesar, partly as a result of pressure against him from the Jewish leaders. The reports after this seem somewhat contradictory and we simply do not know for sure what his future held for him. What we do know is that Pilate, like all of us, must appear before the judgment seat of Christ to answer for all he had done in life whether good or bad. So the next time Pilate and Jesus were in a court situation, in which life and death would be the issue, Pilate discovered who was really in authority that fateful day, when he knowingly, and for selfish reasons, did what he knew was terribly, terribly wrong.

13

Procession to the Cross

Pontius Pilate, the Roman governor, out of fear for his own position, had caved in to the demands of the Sanhedrin for the crucifixion of Jesus of Nazareth. In a vain attempt to exonerate himself, Pilate washed his hands in a public ceremony declaring, "I am innocent of the blood of this righteous man. You shall bear witness to it." The Jewish people answered back, "His blood be on us and on our children." (Some would remember this self-imposed curse some forty years later when the enraged Roman Legions broke down the walls of the city, massacred the population, sparing none, and burned the entire temple complex.)

Before leading Jesus away to the place of execution, the Roman soldiers decided to have their fun with the condemned man who thought he was a king. They took Him to the court of the Praetorium and called together their whole battalion of soldiers to join in the fun. First they stripped Him naked. Then they covered Him with purple cloth (the color of royalty) and placed around Him a purple robe. "But does not a king deserve a crown," they mocked. Taking the limbs from a nearby thorn bush they plaited into a crown of thorns and savagely crammed it down on His head. "But what's a king without a scepter?" they cried. They then took a bamboo stick someone had left lying on the ground, placed it in His hand and kneeled before Him crying out, "Hail King of the Jews!"

To add as much pain and shame as possible, they snatched the reed out of His hand and began striking Him on His head, driving the thorns deeper into His bleeding scalp. There was no pity in these rough and cruel men. They hated all Jews and despised the duty assigned them in this god-forsaken place. They would have their amusement at the expense of this fool they would soon crucify. He seemed to be in great pain from the vicious scourging Pilate had ordered for him, and they were only adding to His pain and humiliation. "Wait till we nail Him on that cross. We'll show him what real pain is all about," they howled.

Just how far was the distance to the cross awaiting Him we are not sure. There is considerable dispute about the exact location. So they led him through the streets of Jerusalem bearing His own cross on his lacerated and torn neck and shoulders. Many of the common people lined the streets to watch the procession. Some, no doubt, joined the mocking and taunting, while the tender hearted women of the city wept as they saw Him stagger along. Seeing their sympathetic tears Jesus said to them "weep not for me, but for yourselves and your children. For the day is coming when people will say, 'blessed are the barren, and the wombs which never bore, nor the breast which never nursed! Then they will say to the mountains, 'fall on us! And to the hills, 'cover us!' For if they do these things to the tree that is green, what will happen to the dry?"

He apparently had used his last bit of strength speaking these words, and had collapsed. When the soldiers were unsuccessful driving Him to His feet with the whip, they compelled a bystander named Simon, (the father of two sons named Alexander and Rufus who were presumably known to the Christian community at the time of the writing of these things) to carry the cross for Jesus. So at last they brought Him to the place He had known all along He must go—to Golgotha. Though beaten and bloody, He arrived there of His own free will. The only things compelling Him were the will of the Father and the desperate need of His sheep, for whom He would lay down His life.

164

14

There They Crucified Him

Jesus of Nazareth had been condemned to death by the highest court of His own nation, the Sanhedrin of the Jews. They passed judgment on Him for claiming to be the Messiah, the Son of God. They willingly ignored the overwhelming evidence that His claim was true. He had healed the sick, fed the multitudes, opened the eyes of the blind, and the ears of the deaf. He had preached the good news and set the captives free. He had even raised the dead to life again. But the corrupt high priests, fearing for their own position of power and wealth had conspired with the traitor Judas and arrested Him in the dead of night. They had tried Him contrary to the procedures of Jewish law and found Him guilty and deserving death.

They sent Him before the Roman governor, Pontius Pilate, demanding that the civil authorities confirm their findings and crucify Him to death. Pilate examined Him again and again. Three times he declared Him to be innocent of the charges, and undeserving of the death penalty. However, when the high priests threatened to report him to Tiberius Caesar for failing to condemn a man who claimed to be king instead of Caesar, Pilate caved in to their demands and sentenced Him to be publicly beaten and put to death by crucifixion.

We know from history that many nations of the ancient world, including Rome, used crucifixion as a means of capital punishment. Several Roman historians refer to crucifixion; none however, attempt to describe it in the details in which many seem to delight. The simple facts are reported in all four Gospels, but again, none of them go into the details of how it was done. Perhaps this indicates that this form of execution was so horrible that it could not be adequately described. The emphasis in the Gospels is not on "how," but "why." This will also occupy most of our attention in this account. However, we feel compelled to give some description of the process, in order that we might more fully understand and appreciate what our Lord Jesus suffered in our behalf.

Let this quote from Dr. William Hendriksen's commentary on the Gospel of John serve to tell the story. "It has been well said that the person who was crucified 'died a thousand deaths. Large nails were driven through the hands and feet. Among the horrors which one suffered while thus suspended (with the feet resting upon a little tablet, not very far from the ground) were the following: severe inflammation, the swelling of the wounds in the region of the nails, unbearable pain from torn tendons, fearful discomfort from the position of the body, throbbing headaches, and burning thirst."

Dr Hendriksen then wisely comments: "In the case of Jesus the emphasis, however, should not be placed on this physical torture which He endured. It has been has been said that only the damned in hell know what Jesus suffered when He died on the cross. In a sense this is true, for they, too, suffer eternal death. One should add, however, that they had never been to heaven. The Son of God, on the other hand descended from the regions of endless delight in the closest possible fellowship with His Father to the abysmal depth of hell…"

The often sung hymn, "O Sacred Head Now Wounded," by Bernard of Clairvaux, as translated by Paul Gerhardt and James Alexander, touches deeply the heart of believers:

> O sacred head, now wounded,
> With grief and shame weighed down,
> Now scornfully surrounded
> With thorns Thine only crown;
> O sacred head, what glory!
> What bliss till now was Thine!
> Yet, though despised and gory,
> I joy to call Thee mine.
>
> What Thou, my Lord, hast suffered
> Was all for sinners' gain;
> Mine, mine was the transgression,
> But Thine the deadly pain.
> Lo, here I fall, my Savior!
> 'Tis I deserve Thy place;
> Look on me with Thy favor,
> Vouchsafe to me Thy grace.
>
> What language shall I borrow
> To thank Thee, dearest friend,
> For this, Thy dying sorrow,
> Thy pity without end?
> Oh! make me Thine forever,
> And should I fainting be,
> Lord, let me never, never
> Outlive my love to Thee.

Why not offer this as your prayer to the Lord Jesus even now, on your knees, with trembling voice and flowing tears?

When Jesus was offered a drug to deaden His pain He refused it, for He would drink the bitter cup the Father had given Him to the last deadly dregs. He would soon know the greater pain of becoming the sin bearer before the Holy Father. So now as the nails were driven into His hands and feet, He would experience the deepest physical pain as well. And He did! He who knew no sin, and was the Father's beloved Son, in whom He was well pleased, now must undergo the judgment and wrath which guilty sinners must endure at the hands of the Holy God. "For He (God) made Him (Jesus) who knew no sin to be sin for us, that we might become the righteousness of God in Him."

The critics of the Bible, even some who claim to be believers in Christ, love to point out what they consider to be contradictions in the exact time of Jesus' execution. In Mark's gospel we read that Jesus was crucified the third hour, which would be nine o'clock in the morning. While in John's gospel we read that Jesus was sentenced to death "about the sixth hour." A number of things must be said about this so-called discrepancy. There was a difference between the Jewish sun dial reckoning of time, and the official Roman way. When John says that the sentencing of Jesus was about the sixth hour, he was undoubtedly referring to the official record Pilate would have been required to keep in his report of the execution. The vagueness of the expression, "about the sixth hour" is logically explained by the fact that in the ancient world sun dials and hour glasses might not be as exact as the demands that modern life places on clocks and minutely perfect computers. It was about nine o'clock when Jesus was nailed to the cross. There let the matter rest, and don't be distracted by such trivial and childish finger-pointing at God's Word by unbelieving folks who look for excuses not to believe the Bible.

For the next six long and terribly painful hours, Jesus lived, suffering and dying, on the cross. When criminals were crucified, they were usually stripped of all clothing and hung naked on the cross. Some records indicate that in the case of Jews being crucified, loin cloths were allowed. At the most, that's all the clothing Jesus was allowed to wear. What of the clothing He wore at His trial, and in the procession to the cross? The soldiers of the execution squad had plans for those. Just after they removed His clothing and had nailed Him to the cross, and lifted Him up, The soldiers began to divide his pitiful few garments. This was apparently the custom, for the men of the execution squad to claim the clothes of the victims. However since the four garments would be of differing value, they would throw their dice to see who would get what of His clothes. When it came to the seamless woven tunic, they decided to have another turn with the dice to see who would win that treasure. It would serve no purpose to try to divide that garment, and would destroy any value it might have. One must wonder, in passing, who had woven that tunic? Was it woven by His mother Mary, or maybe by one of His sisters, or even a grateful follower whom He had healed? Totally unknown to these callous men, they were fulfilling the Scriptures from Psalm 22:18, "They divided my garments among themselves, and for my vestment they cast lots."

At Pilate's orders, a superscription was written and put on the cross over the head of Jesus. It was written in three languages, Aramaic (Hebrew), Latin, and Greek; so that all passing by might read it. Each Gospel writer reported this superscription in a slightly different way, but all giving the gist, in their own words, of the meaning of it. Once more, the critics of the Bible, showing more prejudice than knowledge, see these four different accounts as an example of another contradiction in the Bible. It was, after all, written in three differ-

169

ent languages. The full title was most likely this: "THIS IS JESUS OF NAZARETH THE KING OF THE JEWS. Was this one way Pilate had of taunting the Jewish leaders who had almost tricked him into convicting Jesus? He was certainly sending a message to all who saw it, "Those who would defy Caesar will likewise perish."

This superscription was much more true than Pilate could have possibly imagined. It stands forever as an announcement and a warning. He is the true King, not only of the Jews, but also of the universal kingdom of God. Therefore, to Him God has given "the name which is above every name; that at the name of Jesus every knee should bow, of those in heaven, and of those on the earth, and of those under the earth, and that every tongue should confess that Jesus is Lord..." Most certainly, Pilate will one day discover this to his everlasting regret. He will, in the end, discover what Jesus meant when He answered his question, "Are you therefore a king?" "Yes," Jesus replied, "It is as you are saying that I am a King, for this was I born, and for this I came into the world: that I should bear witness to the truth."

Certainly Pilate did not believe Him or accept His answer. However, he thoroughly despised the Jewish leaders and anything to make them rage in helpless anger he would do. So he ordered this superscription, just to further infuriate them, and to mock them. It worked! The angry demand they presented to Pilate showed just how deeply they were offended. "Do not write, 'The King of the Jews,' but write, 'He claimed to be king of the Jews.'" That this superscription had been written in three languages for all to read and understand was the crowning insult. That anyone should dare think that the long awaited "King of the Jews" was nothing more than a convicted and executed criminal was more than they could take. Pilate delighted in their embarrassment and anger. "They

170

thought they had the power to control me by sending secret messages to Caesar implying that I was not his friend?" "Let them understand they have no power with me." So he responded to their angry demands, "What I have written, I have written, and it shall stand as is." "Case dismissed!"

If what he wrote angered and offended the Jewish leaders, what he did to Jesus caused the Savior great pain and shame. He won his little game of wits with the Sanhedrin and in the process lost his one great opportunity to discover, "What is truth?"

The soldiers having divided up his meager clothing sat down nearby and kept guard of Him who was on the cross. Were they guarding Him thinking He might come down from the cross? Not for a moment did they think that. Were they guarding Him for fear that a large group of Galileans might possible try to rescue Jesus? Probably not. No, it was simply their duty as officers of Rome to keep watch and report when He died.

They were not guarding Him from the scorn and hatred of His enemies. The cross was probably near a well traveled cross roads near the city. At this festive time there would have been many outsiders coming and going from Jerusalem. Most would have heard something about Jesus of Nazareth. Some came to the cross for the same reasons that in the frontier days of the American West, a public hanging was always good for a crowd. Many were at the cross, watching Jesus. Not all of these were enemies. A few, at least, were there to mourn, such as His mother and her close friends and kin. There was at least one of His disciples there, John, to whom Jesus would entrust the care of His mother after His death. But most of the crowd was either callously indifferent, or hostile. Of the latter some sneered and mocked Him as He hung suffering there. They shook their heads at Him and called out, "So you would destroy the temple and rebuild it in three days, would you? If you are really the Son of God, save yourself and come down from the cross, if you're so great."

The chief priests and scribes were there too. They wanted to make sure that this trouble maker was finally brought to bay, and would never trouble them again. (or so they thought) They were sarcastically talking to each other, making sure Jesus would hear them. With mocking voices they asked each other, "Can't this man who claimed to save others save Himself?" They well knew He had saved others. They were present when He raised up the paralytic, healed the lame, opened the eyes of those born blind. They all knew He had actually raised Lazarus from the dead, and they hated Him for it. Now, at the cross, they pretended none of these things had ever happened and were just rumors He had spread. So they jeered and mocked, saying, "Let Him save Himself if He is the king of Israel. Let the 'Messiah', the King of Israel come down from the cross, that we may see and believe Him…He trusted in God that He would deliver Him; let Him deliver Him now if He delights in Him, for He said, 'I am the Son of God.'"

The bored soldiers decided to join in the fun, and they kept mocking Him too. They even taunted Him by offering to Him some of the sour wine they had been drinking, and saying, "If you are the King of the Jews, save yourself."

Then the criminals who were crucified on either side of Him began also to rebuke Him in their painful agony. One of the two especially was berating Him over and over again and saying, "If You are the Messiah, save yourself and save us too!" The other man who at first had berated Jesus grew quiet. He saw the pain and yet the quiet dignity of Jesus. When the Roman dogs had driven the nails into his hands and feet, he had cursed them with all the vile names he could possibly conjure up. The soldiers knew tricks to increase his pain and shut his ugly mouth, and they used every one of them.

He saw them drive nails into Jesus' hands and feet, and to his everlasting amazement and wonder he thought he heard Jesus say, "Father forgive them for they know not what they do." The man, he decided, must be crazy. He heard the sneering crowds deride and mock Jesus, but He did not answer them or rebuke them at all. Maybe some forgotten memory of a long bygone day brought to his mind something he had once read; "He was oppressed and He was afflicted, yet He opened not His mouth. He was led as a lamb to the slaughter, and as a sheep before its shearers is silent, so He opened not His mouth."

A deep pity for silent Jesus began to grow in his soul. He saw and heard the mocking, even from the "holy men". He heard his partner in crime and punishment berating Jesus too. It was too much, even for his sin-hardened heart. He called out to his partner in crime, "Don't you even fear God? Don't you know we too, are under the same condemnation as this man? We are getting what we earned by our misdeeds. This man has done nothing wrong." Strong words indeed for one who was also dying in pain. So often those who are convicted of crimes will loudly protest their own innocence, but this man acknowledged his guilt when he said, "...We are receiving the due reward for our deeds." Then he added even more astonishing words when he said of Jesus, "But this man has done nothing wrong." Contrast this with what the mocking spiritual leaders were saying of Jesus. Had he heard about Jesus? Probably everyone in Galilee and Judea had heard about Jesus and all the amazing, miraculous things He had done. Up to this point this criminal had ignored and ridiculed the stories, but now facing death and whatever lay beyond he was terrified. The conduct of Jesus on the cross, His prayer for forgiveness of his tormentors touch the hard heart of this man, and melted it into repentance. He pled with Jesus, "Lord, remember me, when you come into Your kingdom." Jesus' gracious response assured him that he had asked the right question. More will be said of this in the next chapter.

Standing close by the cross, Jesus saw His mother, His aunt, and two other women, Also named Mary. There also was faithful John, supporting Mary, Jesus' mother. As the oldest son of Mary, He fulfilled His legal obligation to her (according to Jewish law) by committing her to the care of John, and charging John with that care.

About noon of that fateful day, a strange thing began to happen. For the next three hours, until Jesus died, there was darkness over all the land. How may this be explained? What may we make of this? As to how God had brought this incredible darkness over the land, and how extensive it might have been we have no knowledge. Various theories have been advanced as to the "natural causes". They are just that—theories. Of course many just deny this and see it as another attempt by the Gospel writers to dramatize the death of Jesus by adding this unlikely story. All the attempts to explain this unnatural occurrence by natural causes are doomed to failure. A Gigantic thunderstorm of three hours endurance? Not likely. A long lasting desert sand storm or a sudden unexpected eclipse? Also unlikely. The best answer is that this was a special act of the Creator Father to express the more terrible spiritual darkness that "covered the land." Or even more, the terrible darkness Jesus endured when he was cut off from the Father, and became the once-and-for all sacrifice to atone for sin.

Some of the early church fathers such as Origen and Tertullian quoted the Roman historian who made reference to this unnatural darkness in some of his writings. He supposedly also mentioned a terrible earthquake which occurred about the same time. However the value of this should not be overly emphasized.

That this darkness had a special meaning cannot be denied. Once more we quote the words from Hendriksen's commentary on Matthew. "Did it (the darkness) have a meaning?...The darkness meant judgment, the judgment of God upon our sins, His wrath as it were burning itself out in the very heart of Jesus. So that He, as our Substitute, suffered most intense agony, indescribable woe, terrible isolation or forsakenness. Hell came to Calvary that day, and the Savior descended into it and bore its horrors in our stead."

Surrounded and engulfed in this terrible darkness, the suffering of Jesus became unbearable. He knew, that in accepting the "cup" the Father had given Him, He must face the consequences. Now He is experiencing these consequences to the extreme in dreadful suffering of body, mind and spirit. What He experienced in those dark hours is unimaginable and inexpressible. At that time he was "made sin for us, who knew no sin". As "the Lord laid on Him, the iniquity of us all", He cried out in His native tongue, "My God, My God, why have You forsaken Me?" Were these words of great grief also so expressing the pain of both Father and Son for the price paid for our redemption? There is mystery here we cannot explore, express or fully understand.

The final hour was upon Him. He longed for both spiritual and physical relief when He cried out, "I thirst." It would seem the darkness and His suffering had at last reached the hearts of the soldiers carrying out their duty of crucifying Him. Maybe it was the Roman Officer who ordered that one of the men to soak a sponge in sour wine and put it on a stick and lift to His open mouth. But one of those standing by, who did not know the native language of Jesus, thought He was calling for Elijah. So he tried to prevent this act of kindness by saying, "Hold on there. Let's see if Elijah will come and take Him down, and save Him."

At the very end, Jesus said, "It is finished (fully accomplished)." In the upper room with His disciples, during the celebration of the Passover feast, He had prayed to the Father saying, "...I have fully accomplished the work You gave me to do..." This saying was in reference to His ministry on earth, and in anticipation of His work accomplished on and by the cross. So now He said, "It is finished." Then with His last breath, He said, "Father, into Your hands I commit My spirit."

We must now walk very carefully through these next recorded words and events for they are so crucial in understanding exactly what happened to Jesus and even more important, the meaning of it all. All four of the Gospels writers record very carefully the exact moment of Jesus' death. Not one of them say, "And He died." Both Matthew and Mark say that He cried out with a loud voice; indicating that He was still very much in charge of what happened. Matthew and John said, "He yielded up His spirit." This was an act of His will, not that of His executioners. Why is this so important? Had he not said just a few days before this, "No man takes My life from me; on the contrary, I lay it down of My own accord. I have the right to lay it down and I have the right to take it up again. This commission I have received from My Father." Truly, He laid down His life for His sheep. He had finished the work the Father had given Him to do. In the true and full sense of the word, Jesus gave His life up. So the title of this book, and others similar, yet greatly different from it, is misleading. "The Killing of Jesus" or "The Killing of Jesus of Nazareth" are both, in the final sense, inaccurate titles.

Acting on the will of the Father and by His own free volition, Jesus "gave His life a ransom for many."

The Roman centurion who was in charge of the crucifixion crew was moved with deep emotion and great fear. He had observed Jesus carefully during His hours on the cross. He had heard His words. He had experienced the darkness and felt the great earthquake all around him. He was filled with awe and fear. He said, with fear and trembling, "Truly this righteous man was the Son of God."

Meanwhile, before the end, the Sanhedrin had sent messengers to Pilate reminding him that the upcoming Sabbath, only a few hours away, was a special high and holy day, for it was the Sabbath just before the seven day celebration of the Passover. They also reminded him that according to their (Jewish) law a dead body on the cross would defile the land and the holy day. So they requested that the legs of the three on the cross be broken, thus hastening their death. Then their bodies could be taken down and disposed of and there would be no defilement—ceremonially. Pilate agreed with their request. He wanted nothing more to do with these accursed people, so he gave the orders. The Roman guards sent to do this grisly work went from one to another of the criminals and swung their heavy iron hammers breaking the legs and making it impossible for them to push up and breathe. They died within a few moments. Then they approached the cross on which the body of Jesus hung. The centurion who had led the execution stopped them. "But we have orders to break His legs to hasten His death", they protested. "He is already dead, don't you swing that hammer at His legs." One of them responded, "Well we have to make sure don't we?" With that, he suddenly thrust his spear into Jesus' heart, and blood and water poured out. Many articles and even books have been written to explain the words, "There came out blood and water." The main point must not be missed; Jesus was most certainly dead, and the piercing of His heart by the Roman spear proved that beyond doubt. He had given His life by His own will and the will of His Father in heaven.

At the death of Jesus, an earthquake occurred. "The earth quaked, the rocks were split, and the graves were opened." It is not the purpose of this book to further explore the meaning of the following words, but just to note what the Scriptures attest. "And many bodies of the saints who had fallen asleep were raised; and having left their tombs, after His resurrection they went into the holy city and appeared to many." That's really all we know about this except to say that this was another confirmation from the Father that the work accomplished by Jesus was accepted and applied. We shall wait for the full explanation of these things when we meet Him in His completed kingdom!

The rending of the great temple veil is another sign. This one almost explains itself. The veil between the Holy Place and the Holiest of Holies was placed there by God's direct orders through Moses. At the exact moment Jesus died, and from that time on, the way into the immediate presence of God was no longer forbidden. Jesus, the great High Priest had made the perfect and complete sacrifice, and all who take refuge in Him are freely admitted into the presence of the Holy Father.

But what of the body of Jesus? As the evening wore on, and before the Sabbath began at sunset, a man named Joseph, from the village of Arimathea came boldly before Pilate and asked permission to take Jesus, body down from the cross and inter it in his own tomb, which he had hewn out of the rock. Joseph was a wealthy man who was himself a disciple of Jesus, but secretly for fear of the Jews. He is described as "a good and righteous man, a reputable member of the Sanhedrin who had not assented to their counsel and deed." Pilate could hardly believe that Jesus was really dead until assured so by the centurion. He granted Joseph's request and gave him permission to remove the body and bury it in his tomb as requested. Joseph bought fine linen cloth in which to wrap the body of Jesus. About that time Nicodemus joined him with more linen and embalming spices of myrrh and aloes, and together they carefully and reverently wrapped Jesus' body and placed it in Joseph's tomb. Together the two men, disciples of Jesus, but no longer in secret for fear of the Jews, after placing Jesus body in this tomb left the garden where it was located and went away. It is hoped they left to pray for the courage to do what they had feared to do while Jesus was alive. If so they would have a glorious and awesome surprise on the third day.

The others, including the few women who had stayed at the cross 'till Jesus was dead, left sorrowful and in deep mourning. Not the chief priests or the Pharisees. They laid aside their scruples about the Sabbath and went before Pilate with a request. These men who had maintained such a holy reverence for the Sabbath, let their fear and hatred of Jesus overcome their lightly held scruples and went straight to Pilate on the next day. They were going to make sure that this whole matter of Jesus of Nazareth be ended once and for all time. "Sir, we remember that this imposter, while he was yet alive said, 'after three days I will rise.' Command therefore that the grave be made secure until the third day, lest His disciples come by night and steal Him away, and say to the people, 'He is risen from the dead; and the last deception be worse than the first." And Pilate said to them, "You have a guard detachment; go and make it as secure as you can." So they went and made the sepulcher secure, sealing the stone, and stationing the guard." It was the best they could do. It wasn't good enough!

REFLECTIONS
ON THE
SEVEN LAST WORDS
OF CHRIST

1

"Father, Forgive Them."

LUKE 23:26-38

If there was ever any doubt in your mind that Jesus Christ is the Son of God and the Lamb of God who takes away the sin of the world, His final words spoken from the cross in His suffering should remove any and all such doubts. There is so much more here than we will ever fully understand this side of heaven. Altogether these last sayings of Jesus touch on every human need in our fallen condition, and offer hope, firm hope, that God's grace is truly all sufficient to meet our needs in this world, and the world to come.

When one even faintly understands the agony and pain, physically, mentally, and emotionally involved in this most cruel form of execution, and the horror of One who knew no sin being made sin for us, it is a wonder beyond all imagination that our dear Lord spoke any words at all, and even more that He consciously directed His final words in such a way as to be one grand benediction upon His body and bride, the Church.

I find it singularly appropriate that Luke should be the writer who recorded for us the first two of these seven last words. In His Gospel story, Luke was the one who went into such minute detail when writing about the conception and birth of Jesus. He told us things about the incarnation that none of the other Gospel writers mentioned in their narrative. He was so very careful to give a beautiful picture of the encounter between Mary and the Angel Gabriel, and to record her beautiful song of praise, which we know as the Magnificat. In his birth accounts of Jesus, Luke gives many details omitted by the other Gospel writers. The same is true of his detailed account of the trials, the sufferings, the execution, and some of the spoken words of Jesus from the cross. Do you see why it is so important that we have all four accounts given to us? Each Gospel writer shows something of these things the others omit. So we need all four to have a full account of our Lord's sufferings and death. Only Luke reports these words of Jesus, Father forgive them for they do not know what they do, even as the nails were driven into His hands and feet or as the cross was lifted up and dropped into the waiting posthole.

We seek now to comprehend these words by asking a few simple questions.

1. For whom was Jesus praying?
2. What was He asking of the Father?
3. How was this request answered, then and now?
4. What may we learn from these words and how they meet two of our deepest needs?

FOR WHOM WAS JESUS PRAYING?

I believe He was praying for all those who participated in His trials and death. That would include the officers who arrested Him. Do you remember that when Jesus was being arrested, Peter waded into the mob, cutting of the ear of one officer? What did Jesus say and do then? He commanded Peter to sheathe his sword, but even more He actually healed the ear of Malchus, the officer, so we would

184

know those arresting Him were included in His prayer. But did the Sanhedrin members not know what they were doing? To a point, but not the full extent of the baseness and depravity of their judgment.

Pilate came as near as anyone to recognizing the injustice of what was being done, for three times he declared Jesus innocent of any crime at all, but caved in to the demands of the leaders who demanded His death. Were the crowds who chanted and cried out for His death unaware of what they were doing? Were the soldiers who first mocked, abused and tortured Him and then actually carried out the execution not aware of what they were doing? Again we must say, only partially; and in the end, the leader of the squad when he saw of the darkness and all that happened and heard the words of Jesus, said of Him, *Truly this man was the Son of God.*

Every one of these people knew they were doing a terrible wrong. They had perverted justice, despised mercy and proudly killed the Son of God. Yet Jesus prayed: *Father, forgive them for they do not know what they do.* None of these people understood fully what they had done; they had actually killed the Son of God and true Messiah of Israel. I believe Jesus had them all in mind when He spoke these words to the Father. Is there more? Yes, but wait a bit to expand this request beyond the immediate context.

WHAT WAS JESUS ASKING OF THE FATHER?

There are those who attempt to mitigate or even erase these words because of their own pre-conceived notions about the limitations of forgiveness. Some point to the fact that since some manuscripts omit these words, we are free to ignore them. Ah, but many manuscripts do include them, and there is the wider evidence that these words are in keeping with all Jesus taught about forgiveness. Another interpretation is brought forth by some who say that Jesus was really asking the Father to withhold His wrath from all those guilty of His death and to postpone their final, full punishment until the Day of Judgment.

But I believe these words must be taken at face value, without trying to mitigate their force by our own preconceptions. I believe when He said: *Father, forgive them,* He meant just that.

"Blot out their transgressions completely. In Thy sovereign grace cause them to truly repent, so that they can and will be pardoned fully." That is how Dr William Hendriksen interprets these words of Jesus, and I fully agree with him. Let me tell you why. First of all, the grammatical construction of these words is almost identical to words in the prayer Jesus taught His disciples to pray as recorded in Luke 11:4: *And forgive us our sins, for we also forgive everyone who is indebted to us.* In Matthew 6:15, we read: *For if you do not forgive men their trespasses, neither will your Father in heaven forgive you.* In another place, He insisted that we must love our enemies, saying: *Love your enemies, bless those who curse you, do good to those who hate you, and pray for those who spitefully use you and persecute you.*

Would our great Teacher tell us to do what He would not do? No, this prayer from the cross was absolutely consistent with what He taught us about praying for our persecutors.

Perhaps equally convincing proof that Jesus truly meant what He said in this prayer was the example of the martyr Stephen when he was being stoned to death by the same men who had condemned Jesus and demanded His death. Listen to these words from Acts 7: *And they stoned Stephen as he was calling on God and saying, Lord Jesus receive my spirit. Then he knelt down and cried out in a loud voice, Lord do not charge them with this sin.* This, I believe, is

186

probably the surest example and explanation of the words of Jesus when He said: Father, forgive them.

In Isaiah 53 we read these prophetic words concerning the Messiah, *He bore the sins of many and made intercession for the transgressors.* What wondrous love is this, 0 my soul? In His intercession for the transgressors, our Lord asked for their forgiveness with added urgency when He said of them, *They know not what they do.* What amazing grace! What a reminder to us who always want to ascribe the worst of motives to those who do us wrong, with little if any room for grace in our hearts.

HOW WAS THIS REQUEST ANSWERED?

In God's amazing forbearance, the people of Jerusalem would have another generation of grace before the destruction of Jerusalem. During that time, thousands upon thousands would come to faith in the Lord Jesus as Messiah, and the church in Jerusalem would become one of the first centers of missionary activity for the Roman world. The light from some of the brightest stars in the Christian galaxy graced that city—not only the original Apostles, but Stephen and Barnabas, and of all people, Saul who became Paul the Apostle. In Acts 6:7, we read these words: *Then the word of God spread, and the number of disciples multiplied greatly in Jerusalem, and a great many of the priests were obedient to the faith.* I believe all this was at least a part of the Father's answer to this prayer of His Son from the cross.

WHAT MAY WE LEARN FROM THESE WORDS, AND HOW DO THEY MEET ONE OF OUR DEEPEST NEEDS?

If our Lord Jesus prayed such a prayer for those who were directly responsible for His suffering and death, what must be the power of His unceasing intercession for His precious elect whom the Father

187

had given Him in the Covenant of Redemption from before the foundation of the world! I believe there are two great lessons we must learn from this, the first of the Jesus' last words from the cross:

A. Satan often takes his deadly whip and attempts to scourge my guilty conscience with the taunts and fears he uses so effectively, and drives me to the point of hopeless despair by reminding me over and over again of all my sins which truly deserve death and hell. Then, above his strident accusations and their echoes within my own conscience, and even beyond the tormenting pain I feel, I may hear again from God's precious word my suffering Savior say: *Father, forgive them for they know not what they do.* And as Satan is rebuked by God's word, it is as though upon my lacerated back of conscience I feel the healing power of the tears and blood He shed for me. Then I know "There is a balm in Gilead that makes the wounded whole," and so may you.

B. The other issue is this: What right do I have to say of the slights, accusations, being ignored, hurt, the object of anger and spite, "That is unforgivable!" Yes, the hurt is real; it can cause much suffering of body, mind, and spirit; and it may wound my heart and damage my life. But I must remember the prayer of my Savior from the cross. *Father, forgive them for they do not know what they do.*

You may be protesting right now saying, "But you just don't understand how much I've been hurt." You're right of course, but does Jesus not know? Did He not understand how bad things could be when He said: *Love your enemies, bless those who curse you; do good to those who hate you, and pray for those who persecute you, and despitefully use you.*" Was He not serious when He said. So *will My heavenly Father also do to you if each of you, from his heart, does*

188

not forgive his brother's trespasses? Can I claim to follow Him who prayed such a prayer and still refuse to obey this basic command?

But you may protest and explain away your unforgiving heart by putting all sorts of conditions on your willingness to forgive. When Jesus prayed: *Father, forgive them, for they know not what they do,* did He add, *but only if they meet my conditions, and agree with My definitions of what forgiveness means?*

Ask God to give you a forgiving spirit which will enable you to pray that they be forgiven as you have been forgiven by your Father in heaven. Then the prayer of the Lord Jesus from the cross will be answered in you.

2

"Today You will be with Me in Paradise"

MATTHEW 20:1-16; LUKE 23:32-43

And Jesus said, Assuredly I say to you,
today you will be with Me in paradise.

In many ways, this is the most remarkable of all the seven sayings from Jesus on the cross, and once more it speaks to two of
the most basic needs of the human heart: the need for belonging
or community, and the longing for heaven. In another sense, this
was a way for the Savior to express confidence that the Father had
heard His prayer, *Father, forgive them,* for He knew that this man's
sins had been forgiven.

We like to deny that we need anyone else, and we say we are
self-sufficient, but we know that's not true. We need to belong.
Sometimes that longing for heaven lies buried deep in our hearts,
its voice stilled by the temporary pleasures of this world and its
siren call, "It doesn't get any better than this."

Or maybe we're just too busy to think about heaven—or hell, for
that matter. But in the stillness of the night when no one else is
there, when even the television and the Internet have been
turned off, there may come a deep sigh from within your soul

that reminds you how fragile and temporary this life is. Perhaps when it becomes clear that you or your dearest one will soon face death, then like it or not, you must consider eternal things. That's what happened to a certain man long ago who realized his time had come and he had no claim on heaven or anything else but death and hell. We call that man the thief on the cross.

Three men were dying on crosses that day—two who were robbers and probably murderers as well, and another who had been accused of blasphemy, a crime of which all His accusers and the one who sentenced Him to die knew He was not guilty.

THE TWO THIEVES

In their pain and anger, both of the robbers began to revile Jesus with the same angry, mocking words the chief priests, the scribes, the Pharisees and the elders were using in their abuse of Jesus. And what were these hypocritical religious leaders shouting out against the dying Jesus? Just listen: *You who destroy the temple and rebuild it in three days, save yourself. If you are the Son of God, come down from the cross. He saved others, He cannot save Himself. If He is the King of Israel, let Him down from the cross and we will believe Him. He trusted in God to deliver Him, let Him deliver Him if He delights in Him, for He said, I am the Son of God.*

As the pain increased in both these wretches being crucified with Jesus, the anger of one exploded into this blasphemy: *If You are the Messiah, save yourself and us!* But something had been happening to the other criminal. He grew silent, and when the first thief began to revile Jesus, the silent one rebuked his fellow criminal. He admitted his own guilt and said that both of them, the two criminals, were guilty and that their punishment was fully justified.

If you have ever spent much time around people who are in prison, you know that it is indeed a rare thing when a person owns responsibility for their punishment, and admits that justice has been done in his or her incarceration. But for a man who was in the midst of the cruelest form of execution possible to say, *we are being punished justly*, was a sure sign that his repentance was as real as his confession.

He went on to declare that Jesus had been unjustly condemned and was being unjustly punished. (Ironically, Pilate had said the same thing but still allowed His crucifixion.) Repentance led to faith, faith led to open confession of unworthiness, and confession ultimately led to a plea for forgiveness and cleansing.

What had happened to this man? How was such a change possible? I think it began when the horror of reality dawned in his soul. He had been tried by a court of law and condemned because he was guilty. Shortly he would face the ultimate Judge, and he knew that he was also guilty of breaking all the laws of God and thus deserved eternal death and hell. The fear of God fell upon him like a giant boulder and crushed him. The first evidence of this was his rebuke of his partner in crime. *Do you not even fear God, seeing you are under the same condemnation? And we indeed justly for we receive the due reward of our deeds. But this man has done nothing wrong.*

Then I think the first glimmer of hope dawned into his soul when he heard Jesus pray. *Father, forgive them...*" If this man could ask God to forgive those who were guilty of unjustly killing Him for crimes He never committed, maybe He can forgive me for the crimes I have committed. He also had to notice that Jesus did not retaliate with words even though He could have justly denied all their false accusations. And he, like everyone else in Jerusalem and far beyond, had heard about this man and the miracles He performed, even raising the dead.

These factors were means God used in his conversion, but the real reason he changed was that God in His magnificent, sovereign grace had regenerated his dead heart. We can only conclude, that he, like us, had been chosen in Christ from before the foundation of the world, and so in God's way and God's time he came to saving faith.

THE IMPERFECT REQUEST OF THE DYING THIEF

The thief's faith was still small and imperfect, but it was true and genuine. He knew that "Nothing in my hand I bring, simply to Thy cross I cling; naked come to Thee for dress, helpless look to Thee for grace; Foul I to the fountain fly, wash me Savior or I die." So he said, *Jesus, remember me when You come into Your kingdom.*

How much did this man really understand? Where did he get the idea that this man dying next to him on his own cross would have a kingdom into which a dying thief might enter?

The dying thief was almost certainly a Jew, and as such he would certainly have some knowledge of the Jews' expectations of a Messiah and a grand Messianic kingdom at the end of the age. He also seemed to know something about Jesus, His life and ministry, for he said of Him, *This man has done nothing wrong.*

There is something about this man's humble petition which reminds me of the words spoken by the Syro-Phoencian woman who came to Jesus seeking help for her demon-possessed daughter. Jesus told her, *It is not right to take the children's food and feed it to the dogs under the table.* Her response of humility and faith was simply this: *Yes, Lord, but even the little dogs eat the crumbs which fall from their Master's table.* Those words

194

earned from Jesus a glowing commendation for her faith—and the healing of her daughter.

Now here this dying thief expresses an even greater faith in Jesus than the woman's. He was not asking what James and John had asked for themselves—¬the highest place of honor in the kingdom. He knew he was not worthy of any place of honor or even a place. He knew he was a sinner with no claim on Jesus or His kingdom. But he also knew the very name Jesus, meant Savior and as such an heir to David's throne.

These may have been the last coherent words this man was ever able to speak. Soon the pain would overwhelm him, and then at the very last they would come and break his legs so he could no longer push himself up to catch a breath. But while a spark of life and sanity still remained, he called upon Jesus.

Perhaps someone who reads this message today is feeling in despair. Maybe you realize that so much of your life is now past and still you are unsure of your salvation. Please, from within your heart while life and breath remain, call out to Him who gave His life a ransom for many, *Jesus, remember me when you come in your kingdom.*

THE PERFECT RESPONSE OF THE LORD JESUS

Assuredly I say to you, today, you will be with me in Paradise. Jesus' response assured the repentant thief that he would abide in His presence forever. The Lord offered this man abundantly above what he asked or could possibly think. This dying man asked for entrance into a kingdom one day, a kingdom he did not understand but that he hoped existed somewhere in the far-distant future of eternity. But Jesus said to him. *Today you will be with me in paradise.* The thief would not live to see the sun set on this day, but before the day was over, he would be with Jesus in His blessed kingdom.

How many of us understand that today is the day of salvation? Eternal life begins when you come to the Lord and call upon His grace. You don't have to wait until some vague uncertain day or time in the by-and-by. Salvation, assurance, peace--these gifts may be yours even now, for the gift of God which is eternal life brings with it the fullness of God's pardoning love, and acceptance now and forever.

The thief had asked, *Lord, remember me when You come into Your kingdom.* Jesus answered. *You will be with Me.* To be absent from the body is to be present with the Lord. He will acknowledge you before the Father, and where He is, there will you be also.

The story is told of a young king who tried valiantly but vainly to defend his small kingdom against invading Roman legions. After he was captured, he and his wife were brought before Caesar who was afield with his triumphant army. The young king's valor was not honored, and he and his wife were sentenced to die immediately. The distraught young man fell down before Caesar and pled for him to spare his wife, saying, "Only I lifted my sword against you. Let me die for us both, but please release her to return to her family and home."

With many tears and pleas he begged for her life, offering over and over again to die in her place. Finally Caesar was moved by his unselfish courage. He summoned the defeated king and his wife to stand before him and granted them full pardon and released them to return home upon condition of faithfulness to Caesar. As they walked away rejoicing in Caesar's mercy, the young man said to his wife, "Did you see how magnificent Caesar was?"

"No," she replied. "I only had eyes to see the man who was willing to die for me." For all eternity, I believe we will have eyes only for the

196

One who died in our place.

The thief asked to be remembered when Jesus came into His kingdom, but Jesus answered, *Today you will be with Me in paradise.* Let the scholars debate what Jesus meant by the word paradise, but in the context it can have but one meaning: heaven. There are several places in Scripture in which the words heaven and paradise are used interchangeably.

If by grace-granted faith you look to the Lord Jesus Christ and know He died on the cross in your place, you may call upon Him for mercy even as the thief of old called upon Him. Grace, pardon, and salvation you will be granted, but so much more than your mind can possibly conceive. From the moment of that feeble cry, and for all eternity, you will belong to Him and inherit the kingdom prepared for you from before the foundation of the world.

3

"Look! Your Son... Look, Your Mother..."

JOHN 19:17-27

Of all the Lord's words spoken from the cross, these to His mother and to His best friend John are the most poignant and in some ways the most endearing. Yet if we dwell upon this only or even primarily as an expression of a son's loving concern for His mother, I think we will miss much of the importance and power of what He said.

Having said that, we must recognize that one aspect of this exchange is Jesus' active obedience to the fifth commandment. In fact, obedience to each of the commandments may be discerned in His seven last words from the cross.

These words to John and Mary involve so many things. They speak of duty to parents and of concern for dear friends. They speak of compassion for those who suffer, and of a desire to somehow mitigate that suffering. They also speak of relationships and duties beyond our immediate family, and to the recognition that we are members of a much larger and enduring family of faith in Jesus Christ.

No, being a Christian does not negate our obligations to family, it just enlarges the circle of responsibility, and intensifies the reality of duty we have for both our birth family and our faith family.

JESUS AND MARY

There had always been a very special bond between Jesus and His mother. It began with the supernatural conception of the pre-natal Jesus within the womb of the virgin Mary.

I have an idea that there were only three people in the world who knew the true story of Jesus' conception: Mary, Joseph, and Mary's cousin Elizabeth. Of course add to that number one more, Jesus Himself. Mary and her husband Joseph would have several other children, but with Jesus it would have been different: not only was He the firstborn, but He alone was the virgin-born.

It was to Mary that Simeon spoke when Joseph and Mary took the infant boy to the temple for the rite of purification. After thanking God for fulfilling His promise that he (Simeon) would not die until he had seen the Messiah, he warned Mary that a sword would break her heart because of her Son.

Later when Jesus went to the temple as a young lad, presumably to celebrate His bar-mitzvah. He became separated from His parents for three days. When after a frantic search they found him discussing theology with the temple rabbis, Mary rebuked Him for causing His parents such anxiety. Jesus' surprised response was, *But did you not know that I must be in My Father's house and about My Father's business?* Still, He went home and submitted to His parents' authority.

Even in this incident there is an indication that Jesus understood that He had a higher calling beyond family loyalty, and that He placed duty to His Father above even His responsibility to His parents. His obedient response to them, however, was a part of His higher duty to "be about His Father's business."

200

What about the relationship between Jesus and Mary? After Jesus began His public ministry, there is an indication that He recognized that Mary would have to adjust to a new kind of relationship in which He would no longer defer to her will and wishes in all things. As a child under the authority of His parents, Jesus recognized their role of authority over Him, which according to Luke 3:51, He readily accepted: *And He went down with them and came to Nazareth and was submissive to them.* But from the beginning of His public ministry, Mary struggled with the idea that Jesus was no longer under her roof or under her authority.

If you are a parent of grown children, you will understand something of her ongoing struggle. You have to be there for them when and if they need you and ask for your help, but you no longer have a role of authority and control over their lives.

Let me say this gently, but I hope you will hear it well. All too often I have seen the conscious or at best unconscious efforts of parents to control the lives of their grown children and children-in-law. For instance, too often what happens in wedding ceremonies does not reflect the wishes of the bride but of her mother. I know you think that's kind of funny and almost inevitable, but really it is neither. Especially in small towns and rural congregations, many young couples are not free to plan their own holidays or even Sunday dinners because of parental and or grandparental pressure to conform to longstanding customs which are held to be inviolable.

Two incidents leading up to the cross helped prepare Mary for the words she would hear from her dying Son: the wedding in Cana of Galilee and the episode in which Mary brought all the other children with her to the place where Jesus was staying in an apparent attempt to take Him home and "straighten Him out."

At the Cana wedding reception, the host found himself in the embarrassing situation of having run out of wine to serve the guests. When this became known to Mary, who was probably a friend of the family or perhaps a co-hostess, she called upon Jesus, presumably to get Him to do something about the situation. I have no idea what her expectations were, but obviously she felt she was within her rights to help direct Jesus in His ministry.

His response was respectful but clearly rejected Mary's effort to direct Him to her ends. When she said, *They have run out of wine. His response was, Woman, what does this have to do with Me? My hour has not yet come.* He did not address her as "mother." By addressing her as "woman," He was using a title of respect, but nevertheless He was telling her that His ministry direction could not come from her, as He must be about His Father's business. It was necessary for Mary's sake that a radical change in the relationship must occur. Sooner or later, she would have to confess Jesus as her Lord and Savior, but the time was not yet ripe for this change. That He proceeded to perform one of His first miracles in response to the need of the moment was not because of Mary's implied request, but because He chose this time to manifest the glory of who He was and to begin a work of faith in His disciples.

The second incident is almost shocking in that it demonstrated Mary's failure to learn the lesson Jesus was trying to teach her, and that she still thought only in human terms about their relationship. Her attitude was almost shocking in light of all she had been told about her Son by the angel Gabriel. Had she forgotten about the witness of the Shepherds and the wise men, who came to adore and worship Him as an infant? Had she forgotten that Gabriel told her, *He shall be great, and will be called the Son of the Highest, and the Lord God will give Him the throne of His Father David, and He will reign over the house of Jacob forever, and of His kingdom there shall be no end?* Now, here comes Mary with the rest of the family seeking Jesus, presumably with the idea of rebuking Him for His teaching and taking Him home. At least we know from John that His earthly brothers did not believe on Him, until after His resurrection.

So far as we know, on this occasion Jesus did not even talk with His earthly family, although they may have overheard what He said to those around Him. I must assume that they either heard or the messenger they sent in to get Jesus returned and told them what He said. And what did He say? Listen to these words from Mark: *And His mother and His brothers came, and standing outside, they sent to Him and called Him. And a crowd was sitting around Him and they said to Him, Your mother and brothers are outside seeking You. And He answered them, Who are my mother and My brothers? And looking about at those who sat around Him, He said, Here are my mother and My brothers! Whoever does the will of God, he is My brother and sister and mother.*

By these words, Jesus elevated the spiritual relationship to Him above any earthly claims of kith and kin. Without faith in Him as Lord and Savior, none of Jesus' earthly family was truly His kin. He was not repudiating His family; He was saying that in the kingdom, spiritual kinship takes priority over earthly claims. How joyful the Lord's heart must have been when His earthly family joined His heavenly family by acknowledging Him as Savior and Lord.

THE WORDS OF JESUS TO MARY FROM HIS CROSS

Now we come to this truly poignant scene at the cross, for Mary was there. A sharp sword, in the form of bitter nails and a blood-stained cross, was breaking her heart. Surely her grief was adding to His, for He understood what pain she was enduring. And I believe the Savior knows and cares for each grief we experience. *For we do not have a High Priest who is unable to sympathize with our weaknesses, but one who in every respect has been tempted as we are.* So Mary's great grief became His grief—and so has yours. The Lord Jesus was actually doing the greatest thing He would ever do for Mary in dying on the cross to save her from her sins. But He also would fulfill His duty to her as her firstborn Son, for in the traditions of the time it was the firstborn son's responsibility to care for parents in need.

But why didn't He at least call her *Mother*? I think his words to Mary, including calling her *Woman*, was motivated not only by duty but even more by compassion. Mary needed to understand that the death of Jesus was so much more than just a son dying in the presence of a beloved mother.

The first time He addressed her as *Woman*, at Cana, He was drawing a line of demarcation in their relationship but went on to perform a miracle for her benefit and for the benefit of many others. Now, the second time He called her *Woman*, He was performing a far greater miracle for her benefit and for a vast host of others, accepting her punishment and yours and mine that we might truly become the children of God.

Mary would not have completely understood all that was happening or even the full import of His words to her until after His resurrection, when she could look back and see the love and tender kindness Jesus demonstrated to her. She would also see that His suffering on her behalf and that of so many more was God's way of bringing her into everlasting joy.

She would also have a loving "son," John—Jesus' best friend—who was so much like the Son she gave up and who would tenderly care for her the rest of her life. And one day, John would come with her before the throne and worship the great Lamb of God and Lion of Judah, her Lord and her God.

One final lesson I learn from these words of Jesus to Mary: He has infinite love and compassion for all His beloved elect whom the Father had given Him. There are times when I do not understand what is happening in my life any more than Mary at first could make sense of what appeared to be the ultimate tragedy of her Son being taken away just as His life seemed to be getting under way. But in the end, I will be able to look back on all that has happened in my life and affirm that God works all things together for good to those who love the Lord, to those who are called according to His purpose, because He died for me and rose again.

The Cry from a Broken Heart

PSALM 22; MARK 15:34

When our Lord Jesus Christ was dying in pain and anguish on the dreadful cross, He experienced all the agonies of a soul in hell. His physical pain was well nigh unbearable, the mental anguish was unimaginable, and the spiritual pain was beyond comprehending. The pain increased as the hours wore on, and the darkness in His soul was reflected in the strange and horrible mid-day darkness which filled the land. Not since the days of the plagues on Egypt had such darkness been seen or felt. Finally, just before the end, something was added more awful than all the other pain of body, mind and spirit He had endured: He had to experience the terrible wrath of God His Father, when He who knew no sin became sin for us. All the evil and all the sins committed from the day Adam fell in Eden's garden to the end of the world, all the misery of sin's consequences was heaped on Him. God, the holy One, dealt with His beloved Son just as if He had been guilty of all these things and as if He deserved the flames of hell.

Up to that point, our blessed Savior had uttered few words. He had committed His mother to the care of faithful John, He had asked the Father to forgive those who crucified Him, He had promised the thief he would be with Him that very day in God's blessed paradise, and He had groaned that He was thirsty. But then when His

207

soul was made an offering for sin and all our sins were transferred to His account and laid upon His heart, it was too much. He who had dwelt from all eternity in the presence of the Father in perfect unity suddenly found Himself abandoned and cursed, the object of holy wrath.

Then from His broken and crushed heart and from His thirsty lips there came that awful cry of deepest anguish. *My God, My God, why have You forsaken me?* These words were but the beginning of a Psalm of David which the Lord knew from His heart. Other words from this same Psalm were used by Jesus' enemies while He was hanging on the cross. *He trusted in the Lord, let Him rescue Him; Let Him deliver Him if He delights in Him.* Some of the words of this Psalm describe very graphically the physical sufferings of the One who was crucified. *I am poured out like water, and all my bones are out of joint; My heart is like wax; it has melted within me. My strength is dried up like a potsherd, and My tongue cleaves to my jaws. You have brought Me to the dust of death. They pierced my hands ands my feet; I can count my bones. They divided my garments among them, and for my clothing they cast lots.*

THE SUFFERINGS OF DAVID

This Psalm was written a thousand years before Jesus was crucified. How are we to understand the connection? Did David have a mystic vision that spanned a thousand years to see his holy Descendent dying on the cross, and so write these words? No, the Holy Spirit was speaking through David of things which David had experienced to a small degree and described poetically. But He was also speaking through David of things far beyond David's experience or knowledge.

Allowing for poetic exaggeration, David had indeed gone through much disappointment and suffering at many times in his life. As

208

a young lad he was mocked and taunted by his older brothers, es-pecially when he volunteered to do what they feared to do—face Goliath in battle. Then after his great victory over the giant, King Saul became jealous of him, and David had to flee for his life. In his own words, he was but one step from death, surrounded in the wilderness by Saul's warriors and with little hope of escape. After his disastrous affair with Bathsheba, he suffered great mental and spiritual anguish because of the dreadful weight of sin which rested on his heart. Even after being forgiven, the consequences of his sins continued to bear bitter fruit. His daughter was violated by her own half-brother, and he in turn was murdered by angry Absalom. This young man then turned against his father David and led a rebellion in which he sought to disgrace, dethrone and kill David. Still David loved him, and when Absalom was killed, David's heart was broken.

So the anguish described in Psalm 22, though not fully a descrip-tion of David's suffering, was still apropos to his life. We too may be called upon to suffer many things in our own lives and in the lives of those we love. There are times when we may even feel for-saken by God, but nothing can separate us as believers from Him permanently. We may suffer disgrace, intense physical pain, deep disappointment in ourselves and others, mental and spiritual an-guish, and perplexing confusion. Most painful of all is the feeling that God has abandoned us.

THE SUFFERINGS OF JESUS UPON THE CROSS

The Holy Spirit who guided the mind and words of the writer knew that this poetical description of David's suffering would be the actual, literal experience of Jesus Christ when He was cruci-fied. Most of His friends had forsaken Him, and His enemies sur-rounded Him and taunted Him in His great agony. They ridiculed

209

Him and mocked Him with these words: *He trusted in God; let Him deliver Him now if He will have Him, for He said, 'I am the Son of God.'* They added, *He saved others, Himself He cannot save. If He is the King of Israel, let Him come down from the cross. Then, they lied,* "we will believe in Him."

Like wild and bellowing bulls they yelled at Him and mocked His pain and agony. After this they would hurry to the Temple to prepare for the Passover feast, the most holy day of all; for after all, they were the religious leaders, the holy men of their people.

It is astounding that David's figurative language could describe so graphically what actually happened to Jesus on the cross. Such words as "*I am poured out like water and all my bones are out of joint*" describe what really happened to those being crucified. *My heart has melted within me* may well anticipate what some medical experts say happened to Jesus, that His heart ruptured as the immediate and medical cause of death. Other expressions as *My tongue cleaves to my jaws ... they pierced my hands and my feet ... they divided my garments among them and for my robe they cast lots ...* sound more like a reporter on the scene than a prophet long years before Jesus died.

Why was all this written and fulfilled? There are several reasons and one above all others.

1. These things were written that we might see something of the amazing nature of God's Holy Word. Every word is true and all are fulfilled.

2. God's mysterious sovereignty and providence is clearly shown forth. In all these things we see the plan and purpose of God being worked out. Each and every detail of His plan of salvation

was known of Him from before the foundation of the world. When Peter preached his great sermon at Pentecost, he said exactly this: *Jesus was delivered by the determined purpose and foreknowledge of God, and you with wicked hands have crucified and put Him to death.*

3. They were written and fulfilled so that we might fully appreciate all it cost God and His Son to forgive our sins and so that we might have the honor and blessing of belonging to Him.

4. For the last and most important reason of all, we have but to look at the last half of this Psalm. Here we discover the reason above all others: His sacrifice availed! The Savior's terrible suffering was soon over, but the blessed results endure forever. *All the ends of the earth shall remember and turn to the Lord, and all the families of the nations shall worship before You. For the kingdom is the Lord's and He rules over the nations....They will come and declare His righteousness to a people who will be born, that He has done this.* So after the Savior's heart-broken cry as He endured God's holy wrath and displeasure, the sacrifice was complete. He cried, *It is finished. Father, into Your hands I commend My spirit,"* and He died. Then the veil of the temple was torn in two from top to bottom, and the way into the Holiest of Holies was opened forever.

And so we come to that holy place. There is no longer an altar of sacrifice or a need for one. Instead there is a simple table spread with bread and the fruit of the vine, but this table is far more holy than even that ancient altar and the meal we eat together is far more effective for the cleansing of sin. Come, aware of your Savior's sacrifice, His pain, His grief and above all His final victory over sin—*your* sin.

5

"I Thirst."

PSALM 42; JOHN 19:25-30

The agony of the cross was almost over. Jesus had spoken four times since the crucifixion began. The recorded words of Jesus when He reached the very depths of His suffering, when He as the sin-bearer—the Lamb of God who takes away the sins of the world— endured the wrath and curse of God upon sin and cried out, *My God, My God, why have you forsaken Me?* This helps us understand more fully His next three sayings and especially the one that immediately followed this heart-broken cry.

The Lord Jesus had endured hunger and burning thirst while He was being tempted in the wilderness at the very beginning of His earthly ministry, but the thirst He endured upon the cross was even more severe physically and spiritually than anything He had ever endured before. His last food and drink had been the Passover meal the night before. His last sleep had been Wednesday night, if then, and by the time this word of thirst was uttered He was probably burning up with fever, dehydration, and loss of blood. So He cried in deep agony, *I thirst.*

But I think there was more to this word than the physical suffering He endured; I believe there was a spiritual thirst burning within Him too. He had just passed through the deepest suffering

213

imaginable, when total separation from the Father had wrung from His lips and inmost being the bitter cry of One forsaken. As you have heard me say before, this is why we say with wonder and reverence in the words of the Apostles' Creed, "He descended into Hell." Is there a more miserable, devastating experience in all the world than feeling yourself cut off from God? God never forsakes His own, but there are many times when His own feel utterly forsaken and spiritually destitute. And at times we justly feel this agony of separation as we remember the words of Isaiah to Israel, *Your sins have separated you from God.*

Now stop and consider that He was and forever is God's only begotten Son, in whom the Father is well pleased. But when His soul was made an offering for sin. He was cut off from the Father, and there was total darkness in His soul. It was not that Jesus *felt* forsaken—He *was* forsaken, and even worse He was accounted as guilty of all your sins and mine too! I think, therefore, that this word, I *thirst*, was a heart-cry at the deepest level for this separation that caused a spiritual thirst beyond imagination to end, and for the Father's face to shine upon Him once more.

Perhaps this word from the lips of our dying Lord was all of Psalm 42 that He was physically able to utter. In God's providence and under the inspiration of the Holy Spirit, the agony David experienced to a much lesser degree and which he described in this psalm, seems to have been written just for the spiritual agony of Jesus on the cross. Listen again: *My soul thirsts for God, for the living God. When shall I come and appear before God? My tears have been My food day and night, while they continually say to Me, where is your God?*

THE SUFFERING OF THE LORD JESUS DURING HIS LIFE AND MINISTRY

But at the same time, the physical side of His suffering was all too real. In fact, the story of His incarnation and His short life is a story of unbelievable suffering. C.S. Lewis once said that when God the Son became a man, it was a much further step down for Him than if a man became a snail or slug. Lewis went on the say that we share creaturehood with the lowest forms of life because we are both created, but for the Creator to become also a creature was unthinkable—except that it really happened.

He was born of lowly parentage, and who besides Joseph and Elizabeth believed Mary's story of how Jesus was conceived? When He was a tiny boy. His parents had to flee into Egypt to save His life. Upon their return, they settled in Nazareth where Jesus grew up as the son of Joseph the Carpenter. That would not mean abject poverty, but it would mean the level of the peasant population. After His public ministry began, He truly lived a life of privation. The first 40 days were spent in the southern Judean desert wilderness being tempted of the devil and fasting for over one long month. Shortly thereafter, a certain scribe came to Him and said he wanted to follow Jesus wherever He would go. His reply was a summary of those three years before His passion and death: *Foxes have holes, and birds of the air have nests, but the Son of Man has nowhere to lay His head.*

That remained true throughout His short life, and when He was dead they even placed His dear body in a borrowed tomb. He was deprived of family, a permanent home, and a settled life. His travels were all on foot except for an occasional ride in a little fishing boat. When he entered the city to offer Himself as the true

Messiah, He had to borrow a donkey to ride on. His meager live-lihood apparently depended upon whatever contributions some would give Him and His disciples to sustain themselves.

There was another side to His earthly life of privation and want: many simply hated Him without cause except for the fact that He exposed their own shallowness and hypocrisy. His circle of friends was very small, and even His best friends were unreliable when the pinch came. Many for whom He performed mighty miracles of grace and healing cared little for His teaching. All His life He "thirsted" and had so little of all the things we take for granted. Re-ally, no one was capable of understanding Him on a human level.

THE EXPERIENCE IN THE GARDEN OF GETHSEMANE

It is ironic that what led Him into His dreadful "thirst" on the cross was His willingness to drink the cup the Father gave Him. This sounds like a contradiction, but it isn't if you think it through. I doubt that He experienced physical thirst in the garden, as He and the disciples had eaten the Passover meal a short time earlier. But if you think of thirst in terms of isolation, it was truly a burning thirst of spirit. He asked His disciples to watch and pray with Him as He went before the Father to wrestle with the dreadful decision which lay immediately before Him. He even took His "inner circle"—Peter, James, and John—apart from the others so that they might support and comfort Him in His hour of grief. But what happened? Even these faithful three proved unfaithful in His time of need. After the first spiritual battle, He came back to them, weary and weeping, I think, and said, *What? Could you not watch and pray with Me one hour?* Then He returned to face the unbearable again, and once more while He wrestled long in tears and groaning, they slept.

Just what did Jesus mean when He prayed, *O My Father, take this cup from Me?* And again: *If this cup cannot pass from Me except I drink it, Thy will be done.* He was referring to the cross and the pain and shame which faced Him there. He was trying to come to grips with the terrible trauma of suffering the wrath and curse of God against sin, though He Himself was sinless. That experience would be far worse than even the dreadful anticipation which nearly consumed His mind and heart as He prayed there in the garden.

There are times when our fears of an approaching event are worse than the event itself (except for a root canal), but in this case no fear or dread could match the awfulness of what He would go through on the cross. I say again, it was His willingness to drink the cup which made Him so utterly thirsty as He hung on the cross.

THE SUFFERING OF CHRIST ON THE CROSS
BEFORE HE UTTERED THIS WORD

Christ's suffering on the cross was brutal and indescribable. The intensity of that suffering increased each moment and hour He was there. It is not my purpose to dwell on the physical side of His ordeal, but neither can we ignore it in our effort to understand this fifth saying of Jesus. His suffering is handled with a degree of reserve in the Gospel accounts so that we would dwell not on what He went through, but on what He accomplished.

His physical suffering was real and horrible. There is nothing about any of our experiences in this world which would prepare us to even faintly imagine the cruelty of crucifixion. One might ask, "Why did the Gospel writers go into any detail at all?" The answer is that even in the first few decades of the church there were false teachers who tried to convince people that Jesus was not really a man at all but only appeared to be, and that He did not die on the cross. This teaching was tearing the heart out of the Gospel, and some fell for it. The Apostles who wrote the four Gospels saw clearly the need to establish the death of Jesus as a reality. What better way to prove His true humanity than to describe His actual suffering and death? John even went so far as to describe in some detail what happens to human blood when one dies.

But in our Lord's case, the spiritual suffering was far more deadly. The weight of the sins of the world—from Adam until the last living person on earth draws his last breath—was laid on Jesus. We cannot even bear the weight of our own sinful hearts, but Jesus the sinless One became, as it were, Jesus the vilest sinner who ever lived. So there was wrung from Him the cry of the forsaken, and then the cry of a thirst too deep and searing to describe.

During His ministry, the Lord Jesus offered the unfailing water of life on at least two occasions.

In John 4, we read the story of Jesus and the woman at the well in Samaria. I won't go into the whole story, but only the offer Jesus made to her: *If you knew the gift of God, and who it is who says to you, give me a drink, you would have asked Him, and He would have given you living water. Whoever drinks of the water that I shall give him will never thirst. But the water I give him will become a fountain of water springing up into everlasting life.* He saved others from this deadly thirst, but in order to do so, He could not and would not save Himself.

Jesus offered the water of life to the thirsty on another occasion, the Feast of Tabernacles. Among other things, this feast celebrated God's miraculous provisions for Israel in the wilderness, and especially the water flowing from the rock at Meribah. This feast not only commemorated that past event; it also anticipated the outpouring of God's grace on Israel and the whole world. The celebration culminated when the priests drew water from the pool of Siloam and poured it out to remind the people of how God had brought water from the rock, accompanied by fervent prayers for the coming of the Messianic kingdom. At that dramatic moment, Jesus stepped forward and cried out with a loud voice, *If anyone is thirsty; let him come to Me and drink.* There could be no clearer proof that Jesus was offering Himself as the Messiah who would bring blessing upon Israel and upon the whole world. But again. He could only make this amazing offer because on the cross He would cry out, *I thirst.*

His word of grace still stands. He offers the water of life to cleanse our guilty souls, and He offers the water of grace to satisfy our deepest longings for peace and joy. These gifts are ours to claim by faith.

The formula is simple yet deeply profound. Accept His offer by obeying Him when He said, *Repent and believe, for the kingdom of heaven is at hand.* Let this be the song of our hearts:

> *I heard the voice of Jesus say,*
> *Behold I freely give*
> *the living water, thirsty one.*
> *Stoop down and drink and live.*
> *I came to Jesus and I drank of that life-giving stream!*
> *My thirst was quenched, my soul revived,*
> *and now I live in Him.*　　　　(Horatius Bonar)

Come. Drink and live!

"It is Finished."

REVELATION 21:1-8; JOHN 19:28-37

Jesus' strength was failing rapidly. The pain and agony of all that had happened to Him, beginning with His prayer of final surrender to the Father's will in Gethsemane, had brought Him to the very brink of death. But before the end there were yet two more words He would speak: *It is finished, and Father, into Your hands I commend My spirit.* It is upon these words, It is finished, we now focus our attention.

This statement is much more than awareness of approaching death. Listen again to these words: *After this, Jesus, knowing that all things were now accomplished, that the Scripture might be fulfilled, said, I thirst.* His next words were *It is finished!* If we are to understand what He meant by that, we have to interpret the word *finished* by these two previous words, accomplished and fulfilled.

I think there is a very real sense in which Jesus was referring to the entire meaning of His incarnation and the purpose for which He left heaven to enter this sin-cursed world. It would be a terrible mistake to think of these words as words of defeat, or even surrender to death. It was not as if Jesus was saying, *I tried my best but it's over now.* It is not as if He was saying what Elijah said under the juniper bush, totally defeated by life and by the wicked power of Ahab and Jezebel: *It is enough, now take away my life, O Lord, for I am not better than my fathers.*

These are incredible words of an accomplishment so great as to be beyond our understanding. Contrary to all outward appearances, contrary to what the gloating enemies thought, contrary to even the heartbroken despair of His defeated disciples, He had fulfilled and accomplished all the Father had given Him to do. He had defeated death, hell and the devil. And only the triune God—Father, Son, and Holy Spirit—knew what He had accomplished even at the very moment of His death and because of His birth, life and death.

The only thing that seemed "finished" to the outward eye was Jesus Himself. He had preached, healed, taught, loved and lived out a complete obedience to the two great commandments of which He said, *On these two commandments hang all the law and the prophets.* Those two commandments? Love God with all your heart, mind and strength, and love your neighbor as yourself. This He had done to absolute perfection, but that all seemed to be over now. He has been rejected, tried, condemned and executed, and with almost His last breath He said: *It is finished!*

How then can we begin to understand this as a great cry of victorious success in what He had been sent into the world to accomplish? Several sayings of Jesus before the cross help us to rightly understand His next-to-last word from the cross. Let's review several so we may have complete and unshaken confidence today in the victory Jesus announced with these words: It is finished!

THE WORLD/LIFE VIEW OF JESUS DURING HIS EARTHLY MINISTRY, AS SEEN IN SEVERAL QUOTATIONS FROM HIS WORDS

A brief summary of this is His own statement: *I have not come to do My own will, but the will of Him who sent Me.* The entire meaning of His life is wrapped up in these words. In the final analysis, this is also the only thing which will give our lives significance and meaning.

If Jesus had lived to satisfy Himself, He would not have endured all He went through between His conception and His death. In fact, He would never have left His Father's side to begin with! Most certainly He would have lived an entirely different life than the one we discover in the Gospels, and He never would have said: *The Son of Man came not to be ministered unto but to minister, and to give His life a ransom for many.*

Jesus had every opportunity to be the most powerful, popular figure in Israel's history. Everyone was looking for a Messiah, and He was wildly popular during His early days of ministry. The common people were hugely impressed that Jesus was not cowed by the corrupt religious establishment, and they knew He had miraculous powers beyond any prophet in the nation's long history. The news of His healing the sick, His opening the eyes of the blind, and His unstopping the ears of the deaf spread like wildfire, and then before their very eyes He took a few morsels of bread and fish and fed the multitudes on two different occasions. The multitudes were determined to make Him king, by force if necessary, and then—as if that were not enough—He raised the dead! Even the rulers who feared and despised Him had to admit that a mighty miracle had taken place.

Let's face it: Jesus had it made. All He really needed to do was go to the top pinnacle of the temple and cast Himself down before the assembled multitudes who had come to the Passover Feast. Then even the reluctant and unbelieving rulers would not be able to deny His claim to be the Son of God, the Savior and King of Israel.

There was one problem. He had not come down from heaven to do His own will but the will of the Father who sent Him, and it was the Father's will that His Son be the sacrificial Lamb of God who would take away the sins of all those whom He had given to the Son from before the foundations of the world. It was the Father's will that Jesus would be the Good Shepherd who would lay down His life for the sheep.

THE WORDS WHICH JESUS SPOKE DURING
THE PASSION WEEK

Many of His words during that final week support the concept that Jesus by His death had accomplished the will of God, but only two need be set forth to prove the point: words about Him at the beginning of the Passover meal with His disciples, and the words of His great high-priestly prayer.

We read these words in John 13: *Now before the feast of the Passover, when Jesus knew that His hour had come that He should depart out of this world to the Father, having loved His own who were in the world. He loved them to the end. . . .Jesus knowing that the Father had given all things into His hands, and that He had come from God and was going (back) to God.*

The path from the last supper to the cross and to these almost final words of Jesus was one He walked intentionally, with His eyes open to all that would transpire. He had set out on a mission to save His sheep, and He knew it included His death on the cross. So as death was now at hand. He was able to say, *I have done what the Father sent Me to do.* The Good Shepherd had laid down His life for the sheep.

The words of Jesus in His high-priestly prayer add further proof to our understanding that when He said, *It is finished,* He was affirming success in His mission and victory over His enemies, especially Satan himself. Speaking to the Father, Jesus said *I have glorified You on earth. I have finished the work You gave Me to do.* Those words spoken just before He went to the cross anticipated the victory He would win. And now from the cross, He affirmed this triumph: *It is finished.*

THE FINAL, FULL EXPLANATION OF *IT IS FINISHED.*

There is only one way to finally and fully understand what Jesus meant when He said, *It is finished!* In Revelation 22, we read: *Then He that sat upon the throne said, Behold I make all things new. And He said to me, Write, for these words are true and faithful. And He said to me, It is done! I am Alpha and Omega, the Beginning and the End. I will give of the fountain of the water of life freely to him who thirsts. He who overcomes shall inherit all things, and I will be His God, and he shall be My son.*

Our Lord knew that upon His enthronement as King of kings and Lord of lords over the new heavens and the new earth, He would have completed the entire master plan of salvation determined in the Covenant of Redemption.

But for each individual person, one more step is needed. In the words of an old gospel song from long ago comes this claim of confident faith: *'Tis done, the great transaction's done, I am the Lord's and He is mine. (Philip Doddridge)*

That step is a step of faith, an act of surrender of your personal will to the will of the same Father to whom Jesus surrendered Himself in the Garden of Gethsemane.

The work of Jesus on your behalf is completed in one sense when by faith you claim Him as Lord and Savior. In another sense, this work will not be finished until you are made perfect in holiness and have been conformed to His own glorious image. Then you may say, "I am home at last. It is finished!"

7

"Father, into Thy Hands
I Commend My Spirit."

LUKE 23:44-49

Hear once more all seven words our Lord Jesus spoke in His agony upon the cross. How beautifully they all tie together in perfect order. How fully they sum up the entire life, ministry and purpose of our Lord. How thoroughly they speak to every human need. How well they demonstrate our Lord's obedience to the two great commandments as summed up in Jesus' own words. How fittingly they demonstrate the entire meaning of all the other words He had spoken during the three years of His earthly ministry. Hear them one more time, in order:

1. Father, forgive them for they do not know what they are doing.
2. Assuredly I say to you, today you will be with Me in paradise.
3. Woman, look, your son! Look, your mother!
4. My God, My God, why have You forsaken Me?
5. I thirst.
6. It is finished.
7. Father, into Your hands I commend My spirit.

Do you see how it was impossible for Jesus to utter this last saying until He had said the previous six?

What do we hear in these words? We hear the very heart of Jesus. We hear forgiveness, grace and mercy. We hear compassion and care. We hear sacrifice, heartbreak and the deepest agony. We hear suffering and longing. We hear of incredible accomplishment, and finally we hear unlimited surrender to and complete confidence in the Father. What we hear is our own salvation being forever assured in a poignant, brilliant exposition of the word love—*agape* love.

Now let us hear with understanding and appreciation that final word from the cross, a word of total surrender and total trust.

THE PREVIOUS ASSERTION AND PROMISE AS FOUND IN JOHN 10

In this chapter of John's Gospel, Jesus identified Himself as the Good Shepherd. It was then that Jesus predicted His own death, saying *I am the Good Shepherd. The Good Shepherd gives His life for the sheep.*

There are two things you must hear and understand from these words. The first is that Jesus was making it very clear that He would die only for His sheep. Later, He would identify His sheep as those whom the Father had given Him out of the world. If ever a passage of Scripture taught definitive atonement, it is this one. Salvation is a personal transaction between the Father and the Son on behalf of those called and chosen in Christ from before the foundation of the world.

Many well-meaning people think they honor God by proclaiming that Jesus died for everyone. No one with any understanding of God's immense power and love would ever deny that the Lord could have died for all people everywhere and in all ages, but no one who takes the words of the Lord Jesus seriously will stretch His claim beyond what He clearly reveals concerning His intentions.

Only a sentence or two later, the Lord added these words: *I know My sheep, and I am known by My own. As the Father knows Me, even so I know the Father, and I lay down My life for the sheep.* The implications of these words are very clear. The Father and the Son are in perfect agreement in knowing who His sheep are, and that He (Jesus) would very specifically and personally die for them alone.

The second thing to consider is the way in which the Lord referred to His death: *The Good Shepherd gives His life for the sheep. Then He added: Therefore My Father loves Me because I lay down My life that I may take it again. No one takes My life from Me, but I lay it down of Myself. I have power to lay it down, and I have power to take it again. This command I have received from My Father.*

Beloved, these are incredible, saving words! So we hear Jesus saying His last word from the cross: *Father, into Thy hands I commend My spirit.* As Luke notes, He said this with a loud voice, and we begin to understand something of the power of those words.

Jesus did not lose control at the very end and die at the hands of sinful mankind. Instead, He took control even of His own life and death. He gave Himself up fully to the Father for His beloved sheep of which you are one if you trust Him alone for salvation as He is offered in the Gospel.

All of the Gospel accounts of Jesus' death make it very clear that in a sacrificial act of accepting and drinking the cup of wrath the Father had assigned Him, Jesus dismissed His spirit into the Father's care. His body truly died and was committed to the grave, but His spirit was given over to the Father's keeping until the third day when once more it was reunited with His body--a body gloriously transformed and vested with power no human being had ever possessed. One reason this thrills our hearts is that we know our own resurrected bodies will be similar to His in many ways.

Now hear this: When Jesus said, *The Good Shepherd gives His life for the Sheep,* I believe He also meant *and I give them eternal life.* It is not just that our sins were taken away by His death, but life is imparted to us through His resurrection.

Those of us who are older and whose days on earth are nearing their appointed end, may by God's grace and in the name of our dear Savior also say, "Father, into Thy hands we commend our spirits." For us, it will be a matter of accepting God's good timing. For Jesus, it was by His own timing and by His own will, in perfect agreement with the Father's will and appointment, that He said these words.

THE AMAZING RESULTS OF THESE WORDS
OF POWER AND ALL THEY MEANT

1. *The testimony of the Roman centurion.* The Roman officer who led the execution squad heard and saw all that happened on the cross. He saw the way Jesus responded to the taunts of the accusing crowds. He heard every word Jesus spoke, both to man and God. He witnessed the somber darkness which spread over the land, and felt the earth quake. Even as Jesus yielded up His spirit to the Father, the centurion voiced his amazing verdict on all that had transpired: *Truly this was a righteous man who is the Son of God.*

2. *The rending of the temple veil.* Of all the incredible things that happened when Jesus died, the tearing of the veil in the temple was the most dramatic. We dare not miss the significance of this for our salvation and ongoing sanctification. There were two veils in the temple, but the one mentioned here separated the Holy Place from the Holy of Holies. That inner veil excluded

worshipers from God's immediate presence. Only the high priest could go behind that veil, and then only once each year. Each of the three synoptic Gospels makes it clear that this rending of the veil occurred at the moment of Jesus' death. Thus through His death, the way into the heavenly sanctuary was opened.

The temple veil was heavy, and very strong. Only the hand of God could have torn it so completely and so easily, and only God's hand could open the way into His holy presence, which the tearing of the veil symbolized. The next time you read the book of Hebrews, especially chapter 4:16 and 9:19-20, you will have a much clearer understanding of what the Apostle meant by these words.

3. *The end of the darkness*. The Gospel writers make it clear that the darkness lasted from noon until 3 p.m., but apparently the darkness was lifted as soon as Jesus died.

As soon as you understand that He died for you by command from God the Father, the sooner the darkness of doubt and fear will be driven from your heart. The power of His atoning death is the only thing that can break the power of darkness in your life, allowing the everlasting light of salvation to flood your soul and guide you safely home.

Yes, we believers may walk in darkness at times, overwhelmed by our fears and failures, and so deeply aware of our unworthiness. Don't promise God you will never sin again, for you will, but claim the power of Christ's words from the cross and humbly seek a closer, deeper walk with Him.

It is clear that each of the eleven true disciples received the blessed bread and wine from the hand of Jesus. It is also clear that all of them forsook Him and fled that very same night. But praise God that we know they all later returned, chastened, forgiven and restored. And so may you, even now, even here. The way is open because Jesus said. *Father, into thy hands I commend My spirit.*

POSTSCRIPT 1

Christianity is Founded Upon Actual Events

Factual truth is the foundation for faith. Christianity is founded upon actual events which occurred in history and were recorded by reliable and faithful witnesses. From a historian's perspective, you can be just as sure that Jesus Christ rose from the dead as you can be sure that Julius Caesar crossed the Rubicon and made his way to Rome to take over the reins of government and become the first real Emperor. The resurrection of Jesus Christ on the third day following His death can be just as firmly established as a historical event as the fall of Constantinople and the end of the Eastern Roman Empire. The empty tomb is certainly as well documented as the defeat of Napoleon at Waterloo or Lee at Gettysburg.

No matter how adamantly one may insist that the resurrection of Jesus is merely an article of faith, the truth is that when the same historical criteria is applied that is used to establish the historicity of any other event, the resurrection stands the test, and takes its place in the recorded history of the human race.

Another often overlooked but powerful testimony to the resurrection of Jesus of Nazareth comes from hostile and negative sources. This was the reaction of Christ's enemies when news was brought to them, by the Roman guards who were stationed at the tomb of

Jesus, lest His disciples might come by night and take away His body. The Gospels record the reaction of these guards to the earthquake and the sudden appearance of supernatural beings (angels) at the tomb where Joseph had placed the body of Jesus. These men had fainted dead away with fright. When they recovered, they found the tomb empty and went immediately to the High Priest with their startling report. Caiaphas and Annas gathered the Sanhedrin together and quickly concocted a plan to counter-act what they feared would be a terrible blow to their efforts to do away with Jesus.

They gave a large bribe to the guards to persuade them to make up a story that His disciples came by night and stole away the body of Jesus while they slept. They also promised these soldiers that they would make things right with Pilate if he heard the story of the missing body. The very fact they felt it necessary to pay such a large bribe to the guards to persuade them to spread this story is very strong evidence they believed the guard's account of what happened. The Chief Priests were very fearful of the possible consequences if these men told what really happened at the tomb. They tried their best to do what we would call "damage control." Saying all this to you who read this account is very much like "preaching to the choir," because most of you believe in the resurrection. But are you convinced enough to boldly proclaim and defend this great truth of our faith before a hostile and unbelieving world? If believers will not take such a stand, we may as well join the chorus of unbelief. The purpose of this postscript is to help you understand how crucial this truth is and how important it is for Christians to boldly defend it. To do this, please consider how the resurrection affected certain people who were dealing with many of the same problems facing all believers in every age.

We are assured by the Apostle Paul that at one point the risen Jesus appeared to over five hundred people at one time! But I want

234

to look at just three individuals who met the reason Christ. Each one of these three had to face overwhelming difficulties: one was overwhelmed with grief, another by deep doubts, and the third one with his own personal failure. In all three of these cases the Lord answered their need by proving to them that he was indeed risen and alive again.

The first of these was Mary Magdalene out of whom Jesus had cast demons. Is there any more poignant and heart-clutching scene in all the Bible than this? Mary was weeping bitter tears of grief. Not only had the authorities given Jesus over to the Romans to be crucified, but now someone had taken His dead body away and she was unable to do the last thing she could ever do to show her gratitude and love for the Savior—the preparation of His body for final interment. There is something about a woman weeping that touches our hearts to the depth. As a pastor I have witnessed this far too often. A man goes off to war to serve his country and falls on the field of battle. His pains and fears are ended, but those of his wife or mother have just begun. She will weep the rest of her life for many reasons, not the least of which she could not be there to console and comfort him in his dying moments. I have witnessed the tears of many widows whose husbands died long before them, or the more bitter tears of those abandoned by their husbands. The deep grief of Mary Magdalene seems to capture the heart ache and tears of all women for all time. Defeat, anguish, grief and despair had crushed her. Not only was her Lord and Healer dead, but even His poor mangled body had been taken away. For her there could be no closure and no end to her tears.

No doubt the kindly gardener when he came up behind her and gently asked, "Woman, why are you weeping?" Whom are you seeking?" Maybe it was the gentle tone of his voice which prompted her to respond, "Sir, if you have taken Him away, tell me where you have laid Him and I will take Him away." Surely if anyone knew where His body was, it would be the care taker. There was a pause as she turned partly around and strained to see this man through the mist of the early morning. He stepped closer and said simply, "Mary".

Then Mary turning all the way around Him, knew Him and fell at His feet, crying out, "Rabboni!" (Which is to say, beloved Teacher.) She tried to cling to His feet so he would never, never leave her again. But he said to her (gently again), "Cease clinging to Me Mary, for I ascend to My Father. Go to My brethren, and say to them this message, "I am ascending to My Father and your Father, and to My God and your God."

Now she knew. He was indeed alive, the same Lord whom she had known before, but now gloriously alive forever. Death and sorrow had lost its power to control and ruin her life. Now she had comfort for every sorrow she would still face. Now she had joy, wonderful joy that would not be denied. Now she had hope that would not fail. For Christ is risen, He is risen indeed! His words of assurance meant that she too would rise one day and ascend to Her Father and to her God. Her Lord and Savior, Jesus the Messiah, would be there too at the Father's right hand, waiting to confess her as one of His own.

So if you too are trapped in the pit of grief and despair, thinking all is lost, the Risen Savior is ready to reveal Himself to you by His Word and Holy Spirit. He is able to deliver you from the terrible bondage of grief.

There was another to whom the Lord would reveal Himself. His name was Thomas, often called "Thomas the doubter." He too, desperately needed to meet this same risen Savior. His grief was expressed not so much in inconsolable tears, but the loss of faith and trust in the reality of what he had heard Jesus promise for the last three years. When Thomas saw Jesus cruelly abused and executed in shame and pain, all his bright hope and all his faith fled away. He was left with an emptiness and disappointment too deep for words. His former confidence in all the wonderful things Jesus had promised was lost.

"Never again" he thought, never again will I believe that He is going away to prepare a place for me in the Father's kingdom." Never again could he hope for a kingdom of righteousness and joy. How could he, after what they did to Jesus? Now he believed simply this: Jesus had been defeated. When a man is dead, he is dead. Thomas had seen (from afar) Jesus hanging on a cross, His only crown was a crown of thorns they had forced down on His head before they killed Him. He knew now Jesus would never sit upon the throne of David and bring in the glorious kingdom all longed for. There was just too much evidence to the contrary. He had seen with his own eyes and heard with his own ears all that had happened. It was over and gone. He was over and dead. Maybe some of his own friends, or someone else had indeed taken away His body as the High Priest was claiming.

No matter how slender the cord, most Christians still cling to the hope that Jesus was all He claimed to be, and that He was right about heaven and the conquest of death. But when bad things happen and keep going on, forever it seems, and when dark clouds of tragedy invade your life, when "sorrows like sea billows roll", it becomes very difficult and almost impossible to hold on to faith and hope. That doubt, that cynicism would even make sense, except for one thing—"On the third day, He arose again from the dead."

That historical event is well established. Though I never put my finger into the nail wounds in His hand, nor my hand into the spear wound in His side, I hear Him invite Thomas to do just that. I also hear His gentle rebuke to Thomas, "Be not faithless, but believing." Thomas, no longer wishing to "place his finger in the nail prints in Jesus' hands and his hands into his wounded side", fell at His feet and said to Him, "My Lord and My God." Then I hear Jesus saying to me and to all who will believe, "Blessed are those who have not seen, and yet believe." So I say to Him, "Dear Lord, I believe; help Thou my unbelief. By your resurrection, doubts have lost their power to control me, and ruin my joy."

One further appearance of the risen Christ confirms once again how His resurrection speaks to the deepest needs of the human experience. This was his appearances to Simon Peter, who, under pressure, had denied Him the night He was arrested. Let this man tell you how it all came about, and how the risen Savior rescued him, crushed by the realization of his own miserable failure.

'What does the risen Christ have for one who has failed Him so miserably? I was so sure of myself and the deep love I professed for Jesus of Nazareth. I had boldly declared to Him, in the presence of the rest of our loyal band, that even though all would forsake Him and flee, I would follow Him to prison and to death. He had warned me that I would fail Him and I was appalled that he should doubt me. I was so sure that I was stronger in my faith and courage than all the rest. Yet when the unexpected test came in an unexpected way, I actually denied Him three times in the presence of His enemies. The last time it was with oaths and curses I declared I didn't even know Him at all. Just then, in time to hear me deny Him for the third time, Jesus was led out of the palace of Annas and looked down on me as I stood by the fire cursing and denying." I said to myself, 'what right have I to be called His disciple?' I thought that I might as well forget it and go back to my old life again. I mourned and wept in hiding, all day, the day they killed Him. John found me and described the crucifixion and what Jesus had said while dying on the cross. He also told me of the wicked, cruel taunts of His enemies as He was suffering so. He even told me how one of the two robbers, who were crucified on either side of Him, asked Jesus to remember him when he came into His kingdom and heard Jesus promise him that he would be with Him before the day was over. My self-condemnation engulfed me when I heard that. I knew there would be no place for me in that kingdom. With John and some of the others I stayed in hiding all the Sabbath day, fearing for my life and wondering when we too, would be captured.

Early in the morning after the Sabbath, some hysterical women came running to find us in this place of my misery, telling us that His tomb was empty! They also spoke of angelic beings, assuring them that Jesus was risen and that they were to find His disciples, and especially Peter, and bring them the good tidings that Jesus was alive again.

With John, we rushed to the tomb and it was empty and His graves clothes were laid aside and he was not there. With wonder and amazement we left the tomb and called together the others. Judas, we discovered had killed himself in remorse, and we could not find Thomas. We went to a hidden room in a nearby house and talked about what we had heard and seen. Suddenly, He was there with us speaking the word we had heard Him say so many times before, 'Shalom, Peace.' I knew then that He had risen from the dead but I still could not believe He would ever want me back again. I was so ashamed I could not look Him in the eyes. He kept trying to convince us that He was alive and that we were still His loving disciples. We all felt a strange sense of the unreal, and almost refused to believe our eyes and ears, supposing that He was only a ghost. Finally, He asked, chuckling merrily, 'Doesn't anyone have anything to eat around here?' We watched with wonder as He ate and seemed to really enjoy the leftover fish we had been eating. Then, just as he had appeared, he disappeared.

We still were not sure what to make of all this, so we made our way back to Galilee and our old profession of fishing. It was so heart breaking to remember how it had been the first time He called to us. How joyless and empty my heart felt—just as my nets were empty the next morning after toiling in vain all night. So we started back to shore, but someone standing on the sand called to us with the question all unsuccessful fishermen dread, 'Boys, have you caught anything?' We replied with weary and grumpy voices, 'no!' He called back to us, 'Cast your nets on the right side of the boat and you will find some." So we did, and just like that our nets were filled with large fish, but the nets held and did not break in spite of the heavy weight. John said, 'Peter, it is the Lord!' Impulsively I wrapped my coat around me, for the morning was chilly, and swam the short distance to shore. I was weary, hungry and cold, but Jesus (it really was Him), had already kindled a fire and had fishing cooking for our breakfast. We ate in silence, not knowing what to say. At this very same spot, He had told us three years ago to follow Him and he would make us to become fishers of men, and here we were fishing for fish again.

After breakfast Jesus looked right into my eyes, and into my heart saying, 'Simon, son of John, do you love me more than these?' I said, humbly, 'Lord, You know my affection for You. He said to me, 'Feed my lambs.' Again he asked me, 'Simon, son of John, do you

240

love me?' I said again to Him, 'Yes, Lord!' You know my affection for You.' He said to me, 'Shepherd My sheep.' He said to me again the third time, Simon, son of John, do you have affection for me?' I thought my wounded heart would break when He asked that. So I simply answered Him, 'Lord, you know all things; You know I love you.' His answer confirmed my calling once more when he simply said, 'Feed My sheep.'

Then it dawned on me deep in my grateful soul, 'I am forgiven! I am set free from my guilt! I am restored and He wants me to follow Him and fulfill my calling. By His love and the mighty power of His resurrection flowing through me, I will follow, I will obey as long as I live and even unto death!' And Peter did just that and in the end, laid down his life for Jesus' sake. He had the privilege of preaching the first gospel sermon to a large crowd of people, just fifty days after Jesus had died on the cross and had risen again on the third day. Peter had become a "fisher of men". Oh what a catch he made with that first sermon. He landed three thousand...and the net did not break!

POSTSCRIPT 2

The Great Impossibility

Several years ago there was a report of a symposium by a number of prominent liberal theologians who were discussing a paper called "The supposed resurrection of Jesus Christ from the dead." The main points of the paper under discussion were the evidences for this supposed resurrection, which seemed to be very convincing and difficult to refute. The predictable response of these theologians was to concede the paper was well written. However, they were in unanimous agreement that the resurrection of Jesus was nothing more than a myth, or at best an allegory, which expresses hope for some form of life after death and was never intended to be taken literally. One scholar made the statement that the paper was well written and the evidences presented were difficult to refute, but he went on to say that even if the story of the resurrection could be proven, he still would not believe simply because the resurrection from the dead is impossible. Another said that such an event was impossible because it would contradict the known laws of science. Finally, another scholar said that even if he had seen it with his own eyes, he would simply conclude his eyes were deceiving him. All of the men on the panel said that we could still speak of the resurrection because the human race continues to reproduce itself.

After reading this account of that learned symposium, one could only conclude that these "brilliant scholars" were the direct spiritual descendants of the first century Chief Priests, Scribes and Pharisees. Now compare these illogical conclusions to the fantastic sermon preached by Simon Peter on the day of Pentecost as reported by Luke in the book of Acts. Listen again to his words: "Jesus of Nazareth, a man attested among you by miracles, wonders and signs which God did through Him in your midst, as you yourselves also know; Him being delivered by the determined purpose and foreknowledge of God, you have taken by lawless hands, have crucified and put to death; whom God raised up, having loosed the pains of death, because it was not possible that He should be held by death."

In this age of increasing doubt and unbelief, it is so important for believers to join with Peter and stand firmly against the unbelief that the bodily resurrection of Jesus was impossible. It is equally important that we do not attempt to appease unbelief, as some have done, by trying to explain the resurrection as being only a belief that the spirit of Jesus lives on. We reject such patronizing nonsense for what it is. On the other hand, we also declare with joy that it was not even possible for Jesus to remain in the tomb. Contrary to what some may say, the great impossibility is not the resurrection. According to Simon Peter, the great impossibility was for the resurrection not to occur. Why? Because He was the Lord and giver of life, how could death possibly conquer Him? As the One through whom all things were created, including human life, how then could death destroy Him? This was the great theme of Peter's sermon, that God has declared Jesus to be both Lord and Christ; therefore it was impossible for death and the grave to win this battle.

How often unbelief declares that what God has promised and what God has done is impossible. Yet these "impossibilities" form the very foundation of all we believe. That God should create all things from nothing in the space of six days and all very good: "Impossible" cries the fallen human mind. That God the Creator should also become a creature and enter creation by sending His only begotten Son into the world: "Impossible." That He was conceived by the Holy Spirit in the womb of the Virgin Mary and be born of her: "Impossible." God's Son offers life and hope through the miracle of the new birth, and man responds; "How can a man be born when he is old? "Impossible."

Yet through this blessed mystery, God declares sinful man to be justified before Him because of the obedience and death of His beloved Son, Jesus. "That's impossible," is once more the answer of unbelief. God warns us that He will bring will bring a fiery end to this world and that all will stand before Him in judgment: "Impossible" is still the answer of unbelief.

In fact every supernatural act of God in accomplishing the salvation of His people is regarded as impossible by fallen man. The ancient world destroyed by a gigantic, world-wide flood, and all but one family drown in the deluge? "Impossible." The Red Sea parts to allow Israel to escape pursuit by Pharaoh? Manna falls from heaven to feed the whole nation of Israel? Water gushes from a rock in the dry desert? The sun stands still? The walls of Jericho collapse at the sound of Israel shouting? Three men walk unscathed through a fiery furnace? Water is turned into fine wine, one little boy's lunch feeds 5000 hungry people, the lame walk, blind see, the deaf hear, the dead are raised? "Impossible, impossible, impossible" is the frantic cry of unbelief.

But all these mighty acts of God are but prelude to the greatest of all miraculous truth…the bodily resurrection of Jesus Christ from the dead; because it was impossible for the tomb to hold the risen Christ. Once the doubting and fearful disciples of Jesus were convinced by many infallible proofs that Jesus had actually risen from the dead, they truly became world changers, and they preached this glad word with irresistible power.

When you read the writings of the Apostles and hear their preaching, you discover that the core of all they wrote and taught was centered in the historical events of Christ's birth, life, death, resurrection, ascension, and His promised return. Their claim was nothing less than this; that Jesus Christ rose from the dead in the same body in which he lived, suffered and died. Oh Yes, it was a glorious, new, and powerful body to be sure, but still he was their Lord in whom they had trusted and with whom they had walked in close fellowship for three blessed years.

The very fact that these men went virtually unchallenged is a powerful witness to the reality of the empty tomb. It was less than two months after Christ's crucifixion that Peter preached this sermon. Everyone knew about the crucifixion, and some had witnessed His trial, sentencing and execution. It was no secret that His body had been placed in the tomb of the aristocrat, Joseph of Arimathea. Yet it was to these same people that Peter proclaimed the resurrection. No doubt it was common knowledge that the authorities had bribed the tomb guards to say "His disciples came by night and stole the body." And it was not only Peter who claimed that Jesus had risen from the dead, but the other disciples, some prominent women, and hundreds of other people claimed they had seen Him.

Why did not the Roman and Jewish authorities come forward with a dead body to refute these outrageous claims? Why not capture

246

a weak believer and torture him until he revealed the location of the body? Within a few days after Peter's sermon, thousands of people became believers when they became convinced that Jesus really did rise from the dead. Why wasn't this claim shown to be a grand hoax? Why indeed? Simply this: what they thought was impossible had actually happened because it was impossible not to happen. There was no way they could refute this claim, so they were faced with two options. Either they could believe the evidence and the words of these witnesses and accept the Lord Jesus as the true Messiah; or in spite of the overwhelming evidence, they could continue to reject Him and go on in their stubborn unbelief and blindness all the way to eternal condemnation. This was the choice most made and the choice of the vast majority even to this very day. Peter's claim that it was impossible for death to defeat Jesus meant that His resurrection was inevitable. Follow with me again the line of Peter's reasoning:

It was impossible for death to conquer Jesus because he was and is the Son of God. Peter called Him the Prince of life. The evolutionists insist that life owes its existence to blind chance and the outworking of physical laws for which there is no explanation. The word of God tells us that all life which exists has its origins in the great Creator God who made all things through His Son. John wrote of Jesus Christ; "All things were made through Him, and without Him nothing was made that was made. In Him was life and the life was the light of all men." How then could He, in whom was life itself, be overcome by death? Yes, He submitted to the experience of death for our salvation, but to surrender in finality to its power was unthinkable. In fact it was impossible.

Another compelling reason that Peter presented for the impossibility of death's victory was that the Scriptures of the Old Testament predicted his resurrection, and God's word cannot be broken. Once he proved that point, the thousands who heard Peter became convinced. He cited David's words from Psalm 16: "My flesh rests in hope, for You will not leave My soul in Hades, nor will you allow Your Holy One to see corruption." Since it was obvious that David had died and was buried and his tomb was right there in Jerusalem, his words had to refer to the Messiah, and not to himself.

Finally, the life and character of Jesus made His victory over death inevitable. The disciples had found in Jesus utter sincerity and absolute honesty. He never deceived them, never pretended. He was the master of every situation including storms at sea, sickness, demon possession, and even death itself. This same, powerful and honest Lord had not only foreseen his death in every detail, but had always assured His disciples that he would rise from the dead on the third day. "Destroy this temple and in three days I will raise it up again" was his promise to His disciples and warning to His enemies. When they insisted on a sign, He said the only sign they would receive would be the sign of Jonah who came back from his burial at sea in the belly of the whale. He never warned His disciples of His coming death without adding that He would rise again on the third day. No wonder Simon Peter preached, "It was impossible for death to hold Him." That's the great impossibility of Easter and always. It demands of us what it demanded of those who first heard that great sermon on the resurrection: true repentance, and avid active faith. Peter warned those who heard that nothing less would avail. This same sermon also reminds us that anything less from us would be utterly unacceptable.

CPSIA information can be obtained
at www.ICGtesting.com
Printed in the USA
FFOW02n0116180214
3642FF